Tower Hamlets College
Learning Centre
100171

KT-154-946

This book is

Mental Skills

An Introduction for Sports Coaches

Copyright © **sports coach UK**, 2004

First published 1996 © The National Coaching Foundation
Reprinted 2001, 2004

This pack is copyright under the Berne Convention. All rights are reserved. Apart from any fair dealing for the purposes of private study, research, criticism or review, as permitted under the Copyright, Designs and Patents Act 1988, no part of this publication may be reproduced, stored in a retrieval system, or transmitted in any form or by any means, electronic, electrical, chemical, mechanical, optical, photocopying, recording or otherwise, without the prior written permission of the copyright owner. Enquiries should be addressed to **Coachwise Solutions**.

ISBN 0 947850 34 1

Author:
Chris Sellars
Editor:
Penny Crisfield
Sub-editors:
Dr B Hale, Dr R Mace, Dr N Smith

sports coach UK
114 Cardigan Road
Headingley
Leeds LS6 3BJ
Tel: 0113-274 4802   Fax: 0113-275 5019
E-mail: coaching@sportscoachuk.org
Website: www.sportscoachuk.org

Published on behalf of **sports coach UK** by

Coachwise Solutions
Coachwise Ltd
Chelsea Close
Off Amberley Road
Armley
Leeds LS12 4HP
Tel: 0113-231 1310
Fax: 0113-231 9606
E-mail: enquiries@coachwisesolutions.co.uk
Website: www.coachwisesolutions.co.uk

THE LEARNING CENTRE
TOWER HAMLETS COLLEGE
POPLAR CENTRE
POPLAR HIGH STREET
LONDON E14 0AF

Preface

This home study pack will help sports coaches apply basic mental training skills to their everyday coaching practices. Based on sound sports psychology theory, it focuses on how coaches can apply this important knowledge to the training and competition provided for their performers.

The information and activities in this pack will dispel the myth of sports psychology being the domain of people in white coats. It will demonstrate how easily implemented changes to everyday coaching practices can help the performer cope more effectively with distractions, regain and maintain self-confidence and emotional control, and retain commitment to the training and competition programme. It will also help you to create a coaching environment where mental skills can develop.

Four mental skills are highlighted (the 4 Cs):

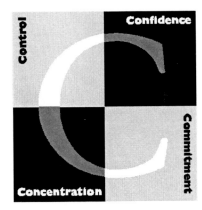

Where further knowledge is required or opportunities to develop specific mental skills, further references are recommended.

Activities are provided to help coaches apply the information to their own sport and coaching situation and consider how their own behaviour affects performers. These will also generate some of the evidence required to demonstrate competence against the coaching standards at S/NVQ[1] Level 3.

If the information in this pack is new to you, it will probably take about 15–18 hours to complete. If you are familiar with material in a particular section, you may wish to skim-read the text, using the activities to check application and knowledge.

This pack is not expected to replace the expert advice offered by accredited sports psychologists[2] but provides some suggestions on how to apply basic information and techniques to your own coaching. If you require expert advice, you should contact an accredited sports psychologist.

---

1   Scottish and National Vocational Qualifications.

2   Accreditation is achieved through the British Association of Sports and Exercise Sciences (BASES).
    For details of accredited sports psychologists contact BASES, Chelsea Close, Off Amberley Road, Armley,
    Leeds LS12 4HP. Tel/fax 0113-289 1020.

Order No:

Class: 100 796.077

Accession No: 100171

Type: REF

Contents

Key to symbols used in the text:

 An activity.

 Approximate length of time to be spent on the activity.

 Stop and consider.

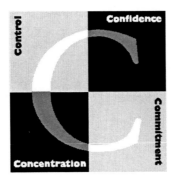

CHAPTER ONE

Introduction

Chapter One: Introduction

1.0 What's in It for You?

It is generally agreed that many factors contribute to sports performance. In addition to the physical, technical and strategic demands of sport, performers must be able to remain focused, maintain emotional control, generate self-confidence, and constantly apply themselves in both training and competition. In your own sport, you will undoubtedly be able to recognise the mental demands placed on performers. Meeting these demands may be relatively easy when things are going well but less so during times of difficulty (eg poor form, distractions, injury).

To help performers achieve these goals, coaches can adapt normal training practices to incorporate a number of simple mental skills – many of which have equal value in other aspects of life (life skills). This does not require the coach to make dramatic changes to existing sessions, but rather to construct sessions slightly differently to create an environment where simple drills and exercises can be developed and where performers are not afraid to try new techniques, and sometimes fail. Coaches may also need to modify their own communication style and behaviour to enable performers to develop the appropriate mental skills.

On completion of this pack, you should be able to:

- explain how psychological factors positively and negatively affect performance in your sport
- identify mental qualities which contribute to good performance in your sport
- explain the role of the coach in developing the mental skills of the performer
- integrate mental training into your coaching programme
- help your performers develop an appropriate mental skills routine for competition[1].

---

1 These outcomes will meet many of the preference criteria in the S/NVQ D12, 13 and 14 units (D6, 7 and 8 for children).

1.1   The Mental Side of Sport

Mental skills are life skills; at whatever level a performer competes, mental skills will improve performance, increase consistency in performance and help the performer cope with difficulties. Mental skills can be used in a number of different ways:

- **Developed as life skills which performers will hone and use throughout their lives.** This approach is particularly valuable for young performers.

- **Used as part of the long-term preparation for a specific event.** This preparation may last several years.

- **Adopted as part of the medium-term preparation for a specific event.** This may be over the duration of a season.

- **Applied as a short-term crisis intervention.** This is only used when a performer or team has a debilitating problem. This should only be directed by a coach trained and experienced in the use of mental skills in sport or by an accredited sports psychologist.

1.2   Mental Skills and Your Sport

In this first chapter you will examine the psychological (mental) demands of your own sport. You will need to identify the key mental factors that affect performers, both positively and negatively, and identify the mental qualities that distinguish good and poor performances.

In particular, by the end of this chapter, you should be able to:

- identify the psychological demands of your sport, both in training and competition

- suggest key mental qualities for successful performance in your sport

- identify the characteristic signs of those with (and without) key mental qualities

- describe how each mental skill assists performance in your sport

- explain the significance of regular mental skills training

- describe the role of the coach in developing mental skills.

It is now common for coaches and performers to refer to the importance of the mental side of their sport. For example, some tennis coaches claim that physical and technical skills contribute only 10% and 15% respectively to successful performance, while the remaining 75% is attributed to mental skills[1]. While this may be deemed an exaggeration by some other sports, it does reinforce the need for coaches to devote time and planning to the mental aspects of their sports. How much time do you currently devote?

---

1   Rowley, S (1989) **Help yourself: Mental Training for Young Tennis Players.** LTA Trust.

ACTIVITY 1

1 Jot down the average amount of time you spend each week in your coaching and training sessions on each of the following aspects of performance in your sport:

- Technique

- Tactics

- Physical preparation (ie fitness)

- Mental preparation

2 Very roughly, calculate the percentage of time you give to each aspect of performance:

- Technical   %
- Tactical   %
- Physical   %
- Mental _____ %
          100   %

Now turn over.

Most coaches would admit that although they believe the outcome of performance is strongly influenced by mental factors, they devote very little time to this aspect of performance in training and coaching sessions (you might argue that it varies according to the age and performance level of the performer). This is often because, with regard to mental skills, coaches feel unsure about what to do, how to do it and even whether anything can actually be done. This pack will overcome some of these concerns and provide you with some practical ways to help your performers develop their mental skills.

1.3   Key Mental Qualities

Each sport places certain psychological demands on performers. For example for the distance runner, it might be the ability to judge pace and tolerate the pain associated with fatigue. On the other hand, for the rifle shooter it might be the ability to block out distractions and control anxiety. For the games player, the main psychological demand might be the ability to make appropriate decisions under pressure at key moments or to maintain focus after an unfavourable decision by an official.

The ability of performers to meet these demands will depend on their mental skills. It is easy to recognise the physical attributes of a performer (eg balance, speed, strength and timing). It may be more difficult to assess psychological qualities (eg concentration, self-confidence, emotional control, commitment) which everyone possesses to a varying degree, yet these are of equal importance.

Just as physical skills can be developed by specific physical training programmes, so psychological qualities can be honed by incorporating specific mental skills exercises. The development of these mental training skills is the subject of this pack.

As a coach, you have to determine:

- which mental qualities are necessary for success in your sport
- the strength of these qualities in each performer
- which qualities need to be developed further to achieve optimal performance
- how these mental skills can be developed
- how your behaviour can influence the development of mental skills.

You will have a chance to tackle the first of these in Activities 2 and 3.

Every sport makes its own unique psychological demands. For example, in tennis you can actually win more games than your opponent but still lose the match (eg 4–6, 6–0, 4–6). It is the ability to win the critical points that matters. In volleyball and basketball, substitutions and time-outs create their own unique mental pressures, and opportunities for coaches to influence players during the competition. In basketball, matches are often won or lost in the last two minutes of a game and quite frequently on the free throw line. In distance events (eg swimming, running, cycling), there are pressures associated with fatigue and the maintenance of concentration towards the end of a long event.

Each sport also provides physical challenges which performers must have the courage to overcome. Having a variety of mental skills helps give performers the confidence to try new techniques and overcome new challenges (eg the 11 stone rugby half-back moving up to the senior game may use imagery and positive self-statements to hone technique and build confidence to tackle 17 or 18 stone forwards).

There may also be occasions in which the performer has some control over the timing of events (eg the tennis server controls when to serve, the rifle shooter when to fire). There is a real opportunity here to implement mental skills strategies to give the performer the greatest chance of being successful. In other situations, the timing of an event seems to be under someone else's control but there may be a fixed period of time in which to prepare mentally (eg the start of a race). In some situations, there is no controllable stoppage time in which to implement mental skills to help maximise performance (eg after falling off the beam in gymnastics, after going two points behind in injury time in rugby).

 ACTIVITY 2

1 Identify critical situations in your sport which appear to create specific mental demands (eg taking or defending against a penalty, being on the blocks, taking on a new opponent):

-

-

2 Identify situations when the performer has specific opportunities to control the situation or timing, which might offer unique opportunities for mental skills to be manipulated (eg at a time-out, at a restart situation in a game, before bowling):

-

-

Now turn over.

---

1   *You have probably identified a number of critical moments in your sport, each of which places particular psychological demands on the performers involved. These demands will vary and draw on a particular mental quality or combination of qualities.*

2   *You may have identified occasions in your sport (and possibly at the critical moments) when performers have the opportunity to use mental skills. It is at these times that mental skills can have a dramatic influence on performance. Identifying these opportunities is the first step in designing a mental skills plan for competition.*

The next activity identifies which mental qualities are essential at these important times.

Many sports have critical moments.

ACTIVITY 3

1 In the left-hand column, list the mental qualities (eg concentration) which are most important at those critical moments identified in the previous activity:

Mental Quality	Positive Effects	Negative Effects

2 For each one, give examples in the second and third columns of how demonstrating or not demonstrating these qualities affects performance in your sport (ie those observable effects that suggest someone possesses or does not possess that particular quality). It may help to think of those critical moments in your sport where the mental skills you have listed are crucial.

Now turn over.

1   You were probably able to cite a number of mental qualities which are important for successful performance in your sport. You may have called them by different names (as shown in brackets), but here are some you may have listed:

- Concentration (attention, focus, not distracted).

- Self-confidence (self-belief, self-assured, superiority, showing courage, not fearing occasional failure).

- Emotional control (being appropriately psyched up, dealing with anger, anxiety, frustration, disappointment, elation, confusion, showing mental toughness).

- Commitment (determination, persistence, dedication, adherence).

These 4Cs (concentration, confidence, control and commitment) are generally deemed important in most sports. However, they may be important to different degrees and at different times.

2   You were probably able to think of a number of occasions when one of your performers displayed these attributes and their performance benefited. Equally, you could probably quite readily think of the potential negative consequences of failing to display the attribute at an important moment. It may help to compare your answers with the following general examples:

Mental Quality	Positive Effects	Negative Effects
Concentration	Able to remain focused after poor first attempt. Able to ignore partisan crowd.	Distracted by poor weather conditions. Not noticing opponent's positional changes.
Control	Controlled anger after being fouled. Remaining relaxed under pressure.	Frustration resulting in poor choice of shot. Muscular tension causing errors.
Confidence	Remaining confident following injury/absence. Willing to take a risk.	Hesitant play and resultant errors.
Commitment	Persevered with new technique under pressure. Continued to pursue season's goals after missing important selection.	Missed training late in season. Lack of effort. Ignoring diet during off-season.

Typically these qualities are interrelated. For example, loss of emotional control generally results in poor concentration (ie focus is directed to the perceived cause such as the official's decision, the player's verbal comment). Similarly, reduced confidence may result in a lowering of commitment. Psychological skills and physical skills also have an effect on each other. To be successful, performers need to harness all their skills – technical, tactical, physical and mental.

For each mental quality, there are a number of mental skills which can be used for its development[1]. The skills described in this pack are relatively simple to learn and apply. However, they will require practise to master. The following panel highlights some key mental skills (note that mental skills can contribute to the development of a number of mental qualities):

Quality:	Examples of using Mental Skills in:
Commitment:	Shared goal-setting
Concentration:	Distraction training Routines and crib cards Segmenting Imagery
Confidence:	Goal-setting Imagery Positive self-talk
Control:	Progressive muscular relaxation Centering Cognitive restructuring

A brief description of each of these techniques is included in Appendix A (page 157). If you are unfamiliar with these, you may wish to stop now and read the relevant section.

Once each performer's strengths and weaknesses have been identified, it is important to devise ways of improving the weak areas and consolidating the strengths. Like physical skills, mental skills are improved by regular practice. With regular practice to promote these qualities, the physical and technical aspects of your sport will improve. This requires time being allocated to adjusting coaching sessions (where necessary) in order to develop and perfect mental skills.

Go back to Activity 1 and check how much time you give to training mental skills.

---

1   For more details of the range of mental skills, you are recommended to attend the **sports coach UK** workshop **Motivation and Mental Toughness**. For details of workshops running in your area, visit www.sportscoachuk.org or contact 0113-274 4802.

Mental skills need to be learnt, developed and become second nature. It is only when they are well practised that they make a genuine contribution to competition performance. The most effective time to develop the use of mental skills is during normal training sessions. This way performers become experienced in utilising these skills while engaging in sport (rather than practising away from the sporting environment). Mental skills can be introduced during the off-season (if your sport has an off-season) but should then be integrated into training, and ultimately competition, as soon as possible.

Mental skills can be introduced in the off season.

ACTIVITY 4

1 Describe the role that you, as coach, will play when integrating mental skills into your normal training sessions (ie how you can help performers with their mental skills):

2 List some initial questions you would need to answer before integrating mental skills into training (eg which mental qualities are a priority?):

  •

  •

  •

3 Suggest ways in which your behaviour may influence the mental state of performers:

  •

  •

  •

Now turn over.

13

1   *Your role is that of facilitator. You should be able to offer a range of mental skills and adapt them to meet individual needs. By making some adjustments to existing training sessions, you can create an atmosphere where performers feel comfortable trying out new mental and physical skills.*

2   *As coach, you will decide when and how these mental skills are integrated into training. To do this, you should consider a number of key questions:*

*   *Which mental qualities are a priority?*

*   *Which mental skills will you integrate into your training?*

*   *How will you adapt training to meet each performer's needs?*

*   *How much time will you need to explain what you are trying to do?*

*   *How will you integrate these skills?*

3   *You may have suggested some of the following (and perhaps many more):*

*   *The method and timing of giving feedback will influence the confidence level of performers.*

*   *Your behaviour before, during and after a competition may affect a performer's anxiety, concentration and confidence.*

*   *The way you determine and negotiate goals with your performers may influence their commitment to training.*

*   *Your ability to adapt your coaching and communication style to the needs of each individual is likely to influence the way in which performers develop and maintain appropriate mental skills.*

1.4   So What?

The following action plan activity will help reinforce and develop the ideas discussed in this chapter.

 ACTIVITY 5

1   Give examples of what you can do now to create a coaching climate which fosters the development of positive mental qualities. Consider how you would ensure that all performers experience:

- regular success

- progressive challenges

- positive support and encouragement (from you and other performers).

2   How will performers be encouraged to:

- develop appropriate technical skills to cope with progressive challenges?

- be creative in meeting these new challenges (eg show flair without fear of criticism, take calculated risks)?

- discuss disappointments with you, in order to identify future goals?

You will be encouraged to review your answers to these questions as you work through the remainder of the pack.

1.5 Recap

Having identified key mental qualities and associated mental skills to enhance them, Chapter Two will provide an opportunity to:

- rate your own and your performers' views of the relative necessity of each quality for success in your sport
- rate your performers' current level of competence and experience in each quality
- develop an action plan to enhance appropriate qualities.

Each of the remaining chapters will examine a key mental quality in turn and the techniques available to enhance them. Each chapter will conclude by encouraging you to develop an action plan for the development of the relevant quality.

This chapter has examined the importance of mental qualities to sports performance. It has also introduced some mental skills which can be used in training and competition to develop these qualities. The remainder of the pack will explore how these skills can enhance performance in your sport.

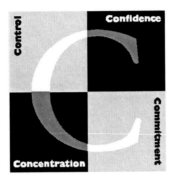

CHAPTER TWO

Performance Profiling

Chapter Two: Performance Profiling

2.0 What's in It for You?

Given that coaching time is precious, it is now necessary for you and your performers to decide the relative importance of each mental quality for success in your sport (ie the mental demands your sport places on performers in terms of these qualities). Performance Profiling provides a way of doing this[1] and of evaluating the current status of your performers in relation to these mental skills.

By the end of this chapter, you should be able to:

- describe the use of Performance Profiling

- use Performance Profiling to assess the relative contribution of each mental quality to success in your sport

- assess your performers on those mental qualities considered important in your sport

- utilise goal-setting to develop those mental skills profiled as important

- use Performance Profiling to develop an action plan for your performers.

2.1 Evaluating Mental Skills

Performance Profiling can be used to assess any aspect of a performer's sporting performance (eg physical, technical and mental skills) and for a number of distinct purposes. The emphasis of this pack is on mental skills and so the contribution Performance Profiling makes to their development will be examined. For example, it can be used to:

- record evaluations of performers' mental skills is an easy to understand way

- compare your views on a performer's mental skills with that of the performer

- compare your performers' current levels of mental skills with targets (goals) for each

- provide information which can help you and your performers plan, and enable you to manage your performers more effectively

- monitor your performers' progress in developing mental skills.

Within any performance in your sport, you can probably identify those critical moments (or components of performance) which changed the course of the event (eg a break of serve, a missed opportunity to score, being boxed in at a crucial moment in a race). It is at these times that a performer's mental qualities are most put to the test. A performer who can utilise mental skills on these occasions will have a better chance of success.

1　For more information, you are recommended to work through the **sports coach UK** audio tape and booklet entitled **Performance Profiling**. For further details contact **Coachwise 1st4sport** on 0113-201 5555 or visit the website on www.1st4sport.com.

Mental skills can help to control frustration.

ACTIVITY 6

1 In the left-hand column, list the typical critical components of performance for one of your performers:

Critical Components	Mental Qualities Rating			
	Concentration	Confidence	Control	Commitment

2 On a scale of 1–10 (10 = most valuable) rate the value of each mental quality to the success of these aspects of performance[1]. List these in the appropriate column.

3 You may wish to repeat this exercise with other performers you coach (this will be used in Activity 9).

Now turn over.

---

1   There are other mental qualities which may be important at these times but the emphasis here is on the 4 Cs.

Performers use their mental qualities at different times and to different degrees. Identifying the critical components of performance for each performer and the contribution made by each quality is the first step in developing an individual mental skills programme (eg for catching the high ball the rugby full-back needs concentration and confidence in his ability to avoid injury if tackled).

The preceding activity has begun the Performance Profiling process. The method of rating mental qualities used in Activity 6 is not visually helpful and does not lend itself well to sharing information quickly with others. Therefore the Performance Profiling *dartboard* is used.

Performers use mental skills at any time.

ACTIVITY 7

1 For each of the critical components of performance identified in Activity 6, transfer your scores to the Performance Profiles below[1]:

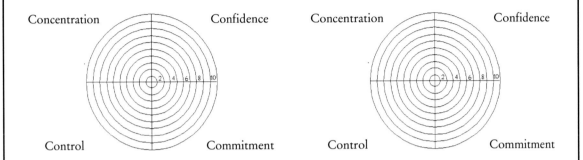

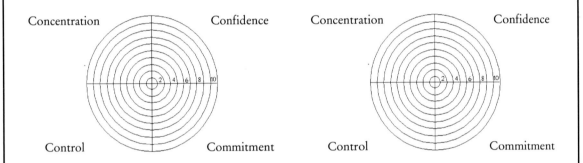

2 Now ask this performer to rate the importance of each mental quality for these components of performance and record these in a different colour on the profiles (or use those provided in Appendix C, page 165).

3 Compare the two sets of scores and list the main differences between them:

- •   •

- •   •

- •   •

Now turn over.

1   More Performance Profile sheets can be found in Appendix C (page 165).

You should now have a picture of the contribution that each quality makes to the key aspects of performance for this performer. On occasion your views may differ from those of your performers. If so, you should discuss with them why this is so and, if possible, agree on the primary qualities needed for your sport.

4   How would you manage a situation where you and one of your performers had differing views on the mental qualities needed in your sport?

Having assessed your own and your performers' views on the need for these qualities, you must now assess to what extent each performer possesses them at the current time.

2.2   Know Your Performers

In order to use the profiles to devise a personal mental skills programme, you need first to assess the performer's current levels of each quality. It is only by identifying the shortfall between desired levels of each mental quality and current levels of these qualities that priorities can be made.

ACTIVITY 8

1   Select two of your performers who differ in terms of their mental approach to sport (ideally one should be the performer profiled in Activity 7).

2   Rate each of them on the following mental qualities (1 = poor, 5 = excellent):

	Performer 1	Performer 2
Concentration	1 2 3 4 5	1 2 3 4 5
Confidence	1 2 3 4 5	1 2 3 4 5
Control	1 2 3 4 5	1 2 3 4 5
Commitment	1 2 3 4 5	1 2 3 4 5

3   Describe how each of these performers behave when they demonstrate
    or show a lack of each quality:

Quality	Performer 1	Performer 2
Concentrates:		
Does not concentrate:		
Shows confidence:		
Lacks confidence:		
Controls emotions:		
Loses control of emotions:		
Displays commitment:		
Lacks commitment:		

4   Compare the answers for the two performers:

Now turn over.

You will probably notice from this activity that no two performers are identical in the way they behave and the extent to which they possess each mental quality. The situations in which they display these mental qualities will also differ, as will the effects on performance (which are the observable symptoms of each quality). This means that it is important to get to know all your performers as individuals.

Think of how two of your performers differ in their ability to perform an important physical skill in your sport. How does the approach to developing this skill differ for each one? How does the method you use to motivate, inspire, challenge, manage and console each one differ?

  ACTIVITY 9

Rate your performers on each of the mental qualities. Space has been left to add others if you wish. Use the ten-point scale which should relate to performers' current levels of each quality. Record the scores on the profiles provided:

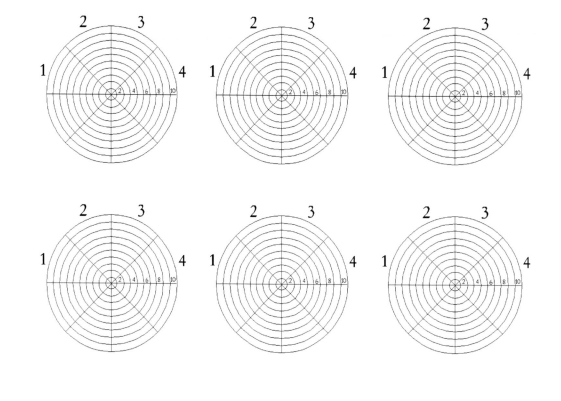

1 = Concentration   2 = Confidence   3 = Control   4 = Commitment

The assessment of performers' current levels of mental qualities can now be contrasted with the relative necessity for these qualities, as identified by coach and performer in Activity 6.

It is helpful to place the three profiles (performer's assessment of the need for each quality, coach's assessment of these needs, assessment of performer's current level of each quality) together to examine where there are discrepancies between them.

ACTIVITY 10

Examine the three profiles provided and describe how the performer's current profile should be improved:

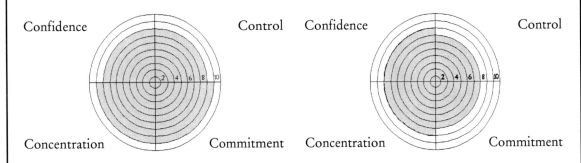

Coach's Ideal   **Performer's Ideal**

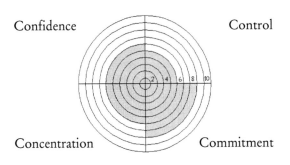

Current Profile

Now turn over.

It is apparent from these profiles that this performer currently lacks concentration and control, qualities rated as important by both coach and performer. If you were this performer's coach, you would need to develop mental skills which would enhance these two qualities.

Try assessing the needs of your own performers in a similar way.

ACTIVITY 11

1 Compare profiles from Activities 7, 8 and 9 to determine which mental qualities need to be enhanced. List these in the left-hand column below:

Qualities to Improve	Occasions Where Needed

2 In the right-hand column, list occasions in your sport where this quality will be needed (this will remind you why they are important).

Activity 11 should now enable you to decide which mental qualities need improving for each performer to be successful in your sport. As with any training programme, you should agree the main objectives (or goals) with performers so both you and they understand what you are trying to achieve and how you are going to achieve it. The information gleaned from Activity 11 will help you identify priorities.

2.3   Goal-setting

Once priorities have been decided, goals and the methods needed to achieve them need to be agreed. Goal-setting is a very powerful tool that coach and performer can use to establish their joint objectives for the training programme. In each of the subsequent chapters, you will be asked to set goals for the mental skills being developed. Goal-setting will only be effective if sound goal-setting principles are applied[1].

  ACTIVITY 12

Think about the goals you set in your sport (either for yourself or with your performers). What are the benefits of setting these goals?

-

-

-

-

Now turn over.

---

1   If you wish to learn how to develop goal-setting skills, it is recommended that you complete the **sports coach UK** mental skills resource **Coaching Sessions: A Guide to Planning and Goal-setting**. For further details contact **Coachwise 1st4sport** on 0113-201 5555 or visit www.1st4sport.com

Goal-setting has many benefits to both the coach and performer. It can:

- *focus attention*
- *direct effort towards the task*
- *help maintain effort/motivation*
- *help performers plan action*
- *help people control their anxiety*
- *monitor, progress and provide feedback*
- *build self-confidence.*

? Think about the goals you could set yourself to create a coaching environment which would foster the development of important mental qualities.

Goal-setting is only effective if it follows the guidelines summarised by the acronym S M A R T outlined below:

• **S** pecific	This is easy to do with sports such as athletics or swimming, where distances and times are easy to assess, but with thought, you should be able to select specific goals for any sport (eg aim to return 80% of serves within one metre of the opponent's baseline).
• **M** easurable	Your goals should be specified in terms which can be quantified (eg aim to complete the first three repetitions in one minute).
• **A** greed	Performers should believe they can achieve goals and agree to work towards them (if they do not, they will not be motivated to try their hardest to achieve them).
• **R** ealistic	Goals should be achievable but challenging (too easy and performers will not give much effort or lose concentration, too difficult and performers will lose heart).
• **T** ime-phased	The achievement of a long-term goal may require a series of shorter-term goals. These should have time scales placed against them (eg aim to achieve 70% success rate within four weeks).

SMART goals should be recorded by the coach and performers.

ACTIVITY 13

1 For one of your performers, set a goal which will aim to develop a mental quality identified in Activity 11:

2 Set yourself a goal to help a performer develop a mental skill in your next training session:

Now turn over.

Check that these goals meet the requirements of S M A R T goals by answering the following questions:

- *Does each goal have an achievable timescale?*
- *How will you know when each goal has been achieved?*
- *How will you share these goals with the performer?*
- *Do you think this performer will be excited by achieving them?*

If necessary, adjust your goals to answer each of these points.

Does the goal focus on a:

- **product** – Does it specify some end result, either in terms of a comparison with other performers or against an absolute standard (eg time, distance, number of tackles)?

- **process** – Does it specify what the performer has to do in order to be successful (eg a golfer to reach forward and upwards as she swings through the ball)?[1]

It is recommended that you consider setting product oriented goals for long-term aims and intermediate goals, or when effort is the key factor. However, process oriented goals are deemed best for short-term goals, especially if skill is the main concern[2].

Mental skills can be used at any time: at rest, in training, before, during and after competition. Developing mental skills in training is therefore only part of your role. Since competition is the focus for most sportspeople, these skills, once developed, need to be utilised in competition.

1   A further description of process and product goals and how they should be used is given in the **sports coach UK** resource **Coaching Sessions: A Guide to Planning and Goal-setting** (details from **Coachwise 1st4sport** on 0113-201 5555) and the **Motivation and Mental Toughness** workshop (details from **sports coach UK** on 0113-274 4802).

2   More information on goal-setting can be gained from the **sports coach UK** resource **Coaching Sessions: A Guide to Planning and Goal-setting** (details from **Coachwise 1st4sport** on 0113-201 5555) and by attending the **Mental Preparation for Performance** and **Motivation and Mental Toughness** workshops. For details of workshops running in your area, visit www.sportscoachuk.org or contact 0113-274 4802.

2.4   Assessing Your Coaching Behaviour

Your coaching behaviour can have a significant effect on performers' perceptions and feelings. It is therefore essential that you assess your own behaviour on a regular basis.

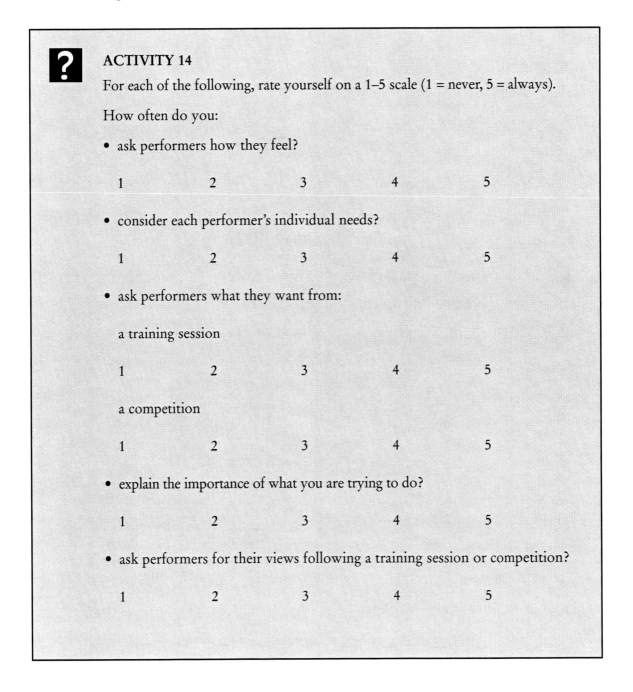

ACTIVITY 14

For each of the following, rate yourself on a 1–5 scale (1 = never, 5 = always).

How often do you:

- ask performers how they feel?

  1   2   3   4   5

- consider each performer's individual needs?

  1   2   3   4   5

- ask performers what they want from:

  a training session

  1   2   3   4   5

  a competition

  1   2   3   4   5

- explain the importance of what you are trying to do?

  1   2   3   4   5

- ask performers for their views following a training session or competition?

  1   2   3   4   5

You also need to be able to assess each of your performers' abilities to cope in various situations. The action plan presented over the page should help.

Action Plan
You may find it useful to profile a number of situations (A, B and C) in your sport in terms of the mental qualities it demands (eg serving for the match or returning to save the match in tennis, settling in the blocks after a false start in sprinting, or sitting on the shoulder of the leader with one lap to go in distance running). You might then profile various performers' responses to these situations and contrast the level of mental qualities displayed with that required.

1 = Concentration   2 = Confidence   3 = Control   4 = Commitment

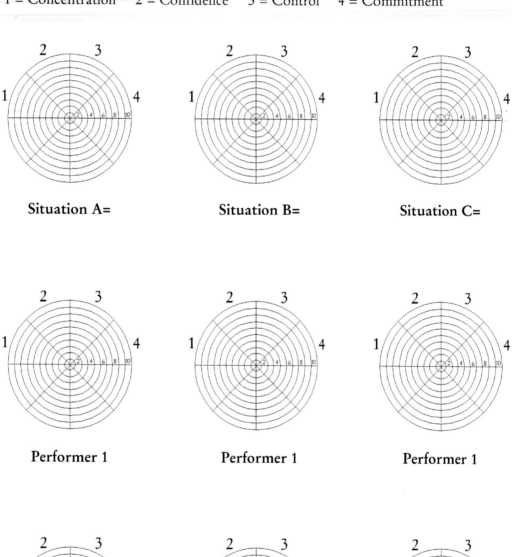

Situation A=   Situation B=   Situation C=

Performer 1   Performer 1   Performer 1

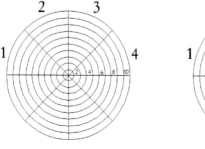

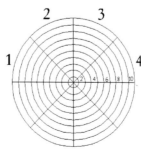
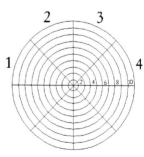

Performer 2   Performer 2   Performer 2

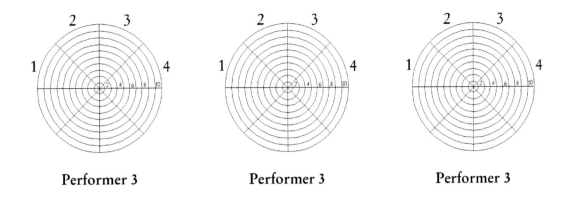

Performer 3   Performer 3   Performer 3

2.4   Recap and What Next?

You should now appreciate that training in mental skills is as important as physical and technical development. You have profiled the needs of your sport and the mental qualities possessed by your performers[1]. Where performers need to develop particular qualities, goals for mental skills can now be set. Each mental skill must be practised regularly, and as a coach you will be able to provide appropriate opportunities for performers to do so. Ultimately, performers must be able to use these psychological skills during competition (and perhaps when you are not present). Therefore, you should help your performers understand how to use these skills to improve performance and cope when things go wrong.

The following will complement information given in this chapter:

Butler, R (1996) **Performance profiling.*** (Tape and booklet.) Leeds, the National Coaching Foundation.

Butler, R (1995) **Employing performance profiling to access performance.*** *Coaching Focus*, 30, pp 6–8.

Crisfield, P, Houlston, D and Ledger, P (1996) **Coaching Sessions: A Guide to Planning and Goal-setting.*** Leeds, the National Coaching Foundation. ISBN 0 947850 35 X.

The following are suggested for those wishing to develop a greater understanding of topics presented in this chapter:

Morris, T and Bull, SJ (1991) **Mental training in sport: an overview.** (BASES Monograph No 3).

Butler, RJ and Hardy, L (1992) **The performance profile: theory and application.** *Sports Psychologist*, 6, pp 27–46.

---

1   If you wish to develop further your Performance Profiling skills or use Performance Profiling for long-term performance monitoring, competition evaluation or group profiling, you are recommended to work through the **sports coach UK** Mental Skills resource **Performance Profiling.**

*   Available from **Coachwise 1st4sport**, Chelsea Close, Amberley Road, Armley, Leeds, LS12 4HP. Tel: 0113-201 5555, or visit www.1st4sport.com

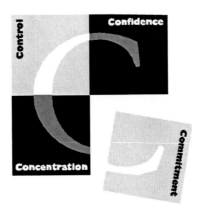

CHAPTER THREE

Commitment

Chapter Three: Commitment

3.0 What's in It for You?

Sports performance depends on participants being committed to numerous goals (eg working on their skills, developing their sport-specific fitness, keeping to an appropriate diet and practising their mental skills). This often requires dedication over many years. The benefits of training will be lost if your performers do not adhere to the training programmes you have agreed.

Developing this commitment to all aspects of training is therefore a key coaching role. By the end of this chapter, you should be able to:

- describe the barriers to adhering to a training programme

- explain the role self-motivation plays in adherence to training

- give examples of strategies for promoting commitment in training and competition

- identify ways in which your behaviour might influence levels of performers' commitment

- develop performers' sense of value

- devise an action plan for promoting your performers' adherence to training.

3.1 Conflicting Interests

Coaches work to help performers achieve their potential. However, most performers have other dimensions to their lives which potentially compete with their involvement in your sport.

 ACTIVITY 15

List possible reasons why a performer in your sport may not adhere to a training or competition programme:

-

-

-

Now turn over.

Non-adherence can be due to any number or combination of factors. Given that performers do not live and train in a vacuum, there are many competing interests and commitments, such as:

- *work*
- *studies*
- *family/partner*
- *friends*
- *social life*
- *other hobbies (possibly other sports).*

Within the sport itself, a performer's adherence can be undermined by:

- *a perceived lack of progress/improvement*
- *not being sufficiently involved in planning the training programme*
- *not understanding the significance of the training programme*
- *not being excited by the programme's goals*
- *getting injured*
- *a lack of enjoyment*
- *anxiety about competition performance*
- *becoming bored*
- *not relating well to the coach*
- *seeing non-adherence or drop-out by friends.*

Recognising and accepting the diverse motives performers have for taking part in your sport[1] and the barriers they face in adhering to a training programme will help you to be sensitive to performers' individual needs, and so cater for them appropriately.

 How often do you ask your performers about their other interests[2] in order to assess potential conflict with completing the training or competitive programme?

---

1   For more information on performance motives, you are recommended to attend the **sports coach UK** workshop **Motivation and Mental Toughness**. For details of workshops running in your area, visit www.sportscoachuk.org or contact 0113-274 4802.

2   This must be done tactfully and without invading the performer's privacy.

3.2   Sharing Your Goals

Goal-setting has already been addressed in Chapter Two (page 29). However, the more strongly performers feel they can achieve a given goal and have a stake in its achievement, the more they are likely to persist, even when things are not going well (ie they will be self-motivated[1]). Sharing goal-setting with performers will raise their feelings of value within the team or group. Performers will also be more inclined to judge success against this target. Shared goal-setting therefore has an important role to play in developing commitment. This requires skill and tact on the part of the coach. Examine the guidelines in the panel below:

Guidelines for Shared Goal-setting

- Discuss why you are setting goals with your performers.

- Explain the need for shared goals and stress the importance of each performer's contribution.

- Provide an overview of the areas to be covered (eg technical, tactical, physical fitness, mental skills, competition).

- For each area to be addressed, coach and performer should agree two or three goals. Short- and medium-term goals should underpin any long-term goals. All goals should be S M A R T (see page 30).

- Differences of opinion should be aired freely and respect for the wishes of the performer maintained.

- Each goal should be placed against an agreed timescale for completion.

- Goals should be written down, preferably made into a *contract* signed by coach and performer.

- A method of monitoring the progress towards these goals should also be agreed.

The way in which this process is managed will vary from performer to performer (and sport to sport), but even the views and wishes of young, inexperienced performers can and should be considered when goal-setting.

---

1   For more information on how to develop self-motivation, you are recommended to attend the **sports coach UK** workshop **Motivation and Mental Toughness.** For details of workshops running in your area, visit www.sportscoachuk.org or contact 0113-274 4802.

Goals should be negotiated.

ACTIVITY 16

1 Draw up some jointly agreed goals (not too many) with one of your
   performers. This might be for a competition, series of training sessions
   or season:

Goal 1:

Goal 2:

Goal 3:

2 Jot down any difficulties you found with devising joint goals:

Now turn over.

How many goals did you agree? If it was for a competition, you should have agreed one or two main goals (perhaps with a few supporting, process sub-goals). More than this and the performer may become confused. For competitions, keep it simple.

For several training sessions or a season, you may have agreed various goals spread over the timescale. Are these goals S M A R T? Look back and check.

Setting joint goals means being willing to listen and adapt, taking into account the needs and desires of the performers. Performers may not be able to express their thoughts as clearly as you, or may expect you to decide the goals for them. You may need to help them express themselves[1]. However, with practice, this process can become part of your ongoing discussions with performers. By empowering your performers to take responsibility for their personal goals, they will better understand them, be more committed to them and strive harder to achieve them.

All goals should be monitored and feedback on progress given to performers. However, the timing of this feedback influences motivation. Generally, you should avoid giving criticism (even constructive criticism) immediately before (or during) competitions or when performers are suffering from low self-confidence. At these times, feedback should reinforce positive behaviour and focus on what is going well. Constructive criticism should be offered at times when performers can focus on making changes to their behaviour without fear of failure. It is also likely to be received better if it is preceded and followed by positive comments (the praise burger). Each performer is unique; only knowing each one as an individual can you judge when best to provide feedback.

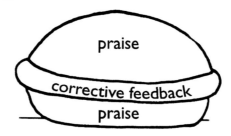

? Think of an occasion when one of your performers was injured or ill. What did you do to support this performer?

3.3   Social Support

However much you help performers to adhere to training and competition programmes, there will be times when they need extra support (eg during times of injury, family or work pressures). At these times, performers will need *social support*; help from those close to them and those with particular experience to offer.

---

1   The **sports coach UK** resource **Performance Profiling** will help you and your performers address areas of common concern.

ACTIVITY 17

For each of the given scenarios, list ways in which extra support can be given to the performer:

- during times of injury:

- during recuperation from illness or injury:

- when suffering a loss of competition or training form:

- during times of conflicting interest (eg during examinations):

Now turn over.

There are numerous people who can contribute to a performer's well-being and provide support. For example:

- *friends*
- *family*
- *work colleagues*
- *medical staff (doctors, physiotherapists, nurses)*
- *team-mates*
- *the coach.*

In the examples provided in the activity, the following may be appropriate:

- ***During times of injury:***
  All medical staff should be encouraged to provide honest and consistent information to the performer regarding their progress. You should maintain regular contact with the performer (unless otherwise requested) and encourage team-mates to do the same. This helps to keep the injured performer involved and maintains a sense of value within the team or squad.

- ***During recuperation from illness or injury:***
  You could pair the injured performer with someone who has recently recovered from injury or establish regular meetings of an injury/illness support group. This can provide moral support to injured or ill performers and provide a model of recovery back to fitness.

- ***When suffering a loss of competition or training form:***
  Goal-setting techniques are important here. The coach and performer should jointly establish a series of progressive goals which strengthen the areas perceived as weak (Performance Profiling[1] can help identify the reasons for a loss of form such as loss of fitness, lack of confidence, technical errors). It is then important that those close to the performer (eg friends, team-mates, family) understand the goals and do not expect too much of the performer too soon. Even when out of form, each performer's contribution to the team should be stressed positively.

- ***During times of conflicting interest (eg during examinations):***
  On these occasions, the coach should be prepared to modify training and competition programmes to accommodate the extra commitments. This should be negotiated with the performer. Again, this can be communicated to those people close to the performer so he/she does not receive conflicting information. The value of the performer as a person should always be upheld.

These are meant as examples of what can be done. Coaches should see themselves as part (albeit an important part) of the support process offered to performers. Consideration of and for others close to your performers will help to prevent perceived conflict and confusion.

---

1   You may need to refer back to Chapter Two.

3.4 Implications for Your Coaching

Your coaching behaviour can have a significant influence on performers' commitment to your sport. This chapter has already identified the importance of self-motivation (Page 41); the way you interact with performers can increase or decrease this motivation.

? **ACTIVITY 18**

Answer the following questions in relation to your own coaching behaviour. They are meant to help you assess your interaction with performers; there are no right or wrong answers, and no feedback is provided.

- To what extent do you *control* the coaching environment (ie who makes the decisions, decides activities, determines priorities, provides feedback)?

  Not at all   Totally

  | 1 | 2 | 3 | 4 | 5 | 6 | 7 | 8 | 9 | 10 |

- How much responsibility do your performers have for their own:

  training behaviour?

  None   Total

  | 1 | 2 | 3 | 4 | 5 | 6 | 7 | 8 | 9 | 10 |

  competition-day behaviour?

  None   Total

  | 1 | 2 | 3 | 4 | 5 | 6 | 7 | 8 | 9 | 10 |

- How often do performers have *fun* during training sessions?

  Never   Always

  | 1 | 2 | 3 | 4 | 5 | 6 | 7 | 8 | 9 | 10 |

- How often do you have fun during training sessions?

  Never   Always

  | 1 | 2 | 3 | 4 | 5 | 6 | 7 | 8 | 9 | 10 |

- What is the nature of the feedback/reinforcement you generally give to performers?

  All criticism   All praise

  | 1 | 2 | 3 | 4 | 5 | 6 | 7 | 8 | 9 | 10 |

Now turn over.

- Do you generally give feedback to performers:

  during and after training sessions?

  during and after competitions?

- To what extent are you prepared to alter training sessions from the prescribed programme?

  What would cause you to do this?

- To what extent do you feel your behaviour encourages performers to be self-motivated and take responsibility for their own behaviour?

Remember: your behaviour can have a significant influence on performers commitment to training and competition.

Action Plan
Select one of your performers who has difficulty adhering to the training (or competition) programme. Examine the reasons for this and with the performer identify ways in which you can offer support. Negotiate goals to help the performer adhere. Implement this strategy, monitor its progress and evaluate its success.

3.5   Recap and What Next?

This chapter has looked at the ways in which the coach and others can help performers adhere to their training and competition programmes. An acceptance of other interests, which on occasions may conflict with your sport, was encouraged and strategies for developing commitment were devised. Conflicts experienced by performers were identified and methods for supporting performers through difficult times examined.

The following will complement information given in this chapter:

Crisfield, P, Houlston, D and Ledger, P (1996) **Coaching Sessions: A Guide to Planning and Goal-setting.**
Leeds, The National Coaching Foundation. ISBN 0 947850 35 X.

Martens, R (1987) **Coaches' guide to sports psychology.** Champaign IL, Human Kinetics. ISBN 0 87322 022 6.

The following are suggested for those wishing to develop a greater understanding of topics presented in this chapter:

Bull, E (1991) **Personal and situational influences on adherence to mental skills training.** *Journal of Sports and Exercise Psychology* 13, pp 121–132.

Duda, J (1989) **Goal perspectives, participation and persistence in sport.** *International Journal of Sports Psychology* 20, pp 24–56.

Gould, D (1986) **Goal-setting for peak performance.** In William, JM, *Applied Sports Psychology.* Palo Alto, CA, Mayfield. ISBN 0 76741 747 X.

Roberts, GC (1995) **Motivation in sport and exercise.** Champaign IL, Human Kinetics. ISBN 0 87322 876 6.

The **sports coach UK** workshop **Motivation and Mental Toughness** may be useful. For details of workshops running in your area visit www.sportscoachuk.org or contact 0113-274 4802.

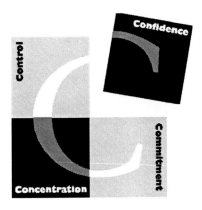

CHAPTER FOUR

Self-confidence

Chapter Four: Self-confidence

4.0   What's in It for You?

Self-confidence helps performers and coaches alike to feel good about themselves and overcome anxiety about the tasks they face. It allows them to try new tasks and overcome difficult challenges. This in turn leads to better and more consistent performances. A coach who can promote self-confidence in performers will not only make the sport more enjoyable for them, but will ultimately improve their results.

This chapter looks at the concept of self-confidence, how it affects performance and what the coach can do to develop it. By the end of this chapter, you should be able to:

- describe self-confidence
- explain how self-confidence affects performance in your sport
- identify the factors in your sport that contribute to high and low self-confidence
- evaluate the self-confidence of your performers
- identify training strategies in your sport to improve self-confidence
- identify techniques to maintain or build self-confidence immediately before, during and after competition
- identify ways in which your behaviour and coaching style can influence the self-confidence of performers
- design an action plan to build the self-confidence of one of your performers.

4.1   What is Self-confidence?

Two sports psychologists, Bunker and Williams (1986), observed the following:

> *The most consistent finding in peak-performance literature is the direct correlation between self-confidence and success. Athletes (performers) who are truly outstanding are self-confident.*

Confidence (and anxiety, the factor that often undermines it) results from the comparison people make between their abilities and the demands of the task they face. If performers feel they can achieve a goal (eg win the next point, achieve a certain score, time or distance, perfect a technique), they will feel confident and probably less anxious. The more success that performers experience in similar tasks, the more confidence they will have. There is therefore a reciprocal relationship between self-confidence and performance:

Self-confidence   Performance

Self-confidence allows the performer to stay positive and in control, even when things are not going to plan.

53

Self-confidence allows the performer to stay positive and in control.

ACTIVITY 19

1 Think about the demands of your coaching and the knowledge, skills and experience you need to meet those demands. List these factors below and for each one, rate your confidence in your ability to meet the demand (1=lowest, 5=highest). One example has been given to help you:

Factor:	Confidence rating:
Ability to change a game plan to meet changing circumstances in basketball.	1 ② 3 4 5
•	1 2 3 4 5
•	1 2 3 4 5
•	1 2 3 4 5
•	1 2 3 4 5
•	1 2 3 4 5
•	1 2 3 4 5
•	1 2 3 4 5

2 If you scored 5 for any of these qualities, list the factors that make you feel confident:

   •

   •

   •

3 If you scored less than 5, what would make you more confident?

   •

   •

   •

Now turn over.

1   *The scores you have given yourself may reflect your current confidence level in relation to coaching (similarly you can probably think of performers whose general personality is not one of confidence, but who are confident in their sporting endeavours) or a more general confidence trait (a more lasting aspect of your personality). Whichever is the case, it is important to remember that self-confidence can be improved.*

2/3 *You may have listed a number of factors that affect your confidence. Typically, the following are cited as factors affecting confidence in sport:*

- *Previous success (or failure).*

- *Being told you are a good (or poor) performer or coach.*

- *Seeing others overcoming (or failing to overcome) problems which you yourself face such as mastering a new technique, or returning to fitness after injury.*

- *Having a positive interpretation of your own motivational state.*

Coaching sessions should provide an environment where these influences occur and positive feelings of confidence are fostered. Given that performance has a major effect on self-confidence, coaching sessions and competitions need to be structured so that performers regularly experience some success (as perceived by them). This may mean altering the rate of progression through a training programme (eg spending more time on certain techniques than originally planned).

Note the importance of performers' *perceptions*: even when performers are successful in your eyes, they need to feel they have been successful. The feedback they receive from you (and important others – performers, family, friends) can completely change their perceptions of ability and self-worth and so boost or damage self-confidence.

 How do you:

- alter your use of praise and criticism to ensure each performer's self-confidence is maintained?

- decide when to give feedback to each performer?

- help performers cope with disappointments?

- make each of your performers feel important?

4.2 Assessing Self-confidence

Try a similar exercise to Activity 19 with two or three of your performers.

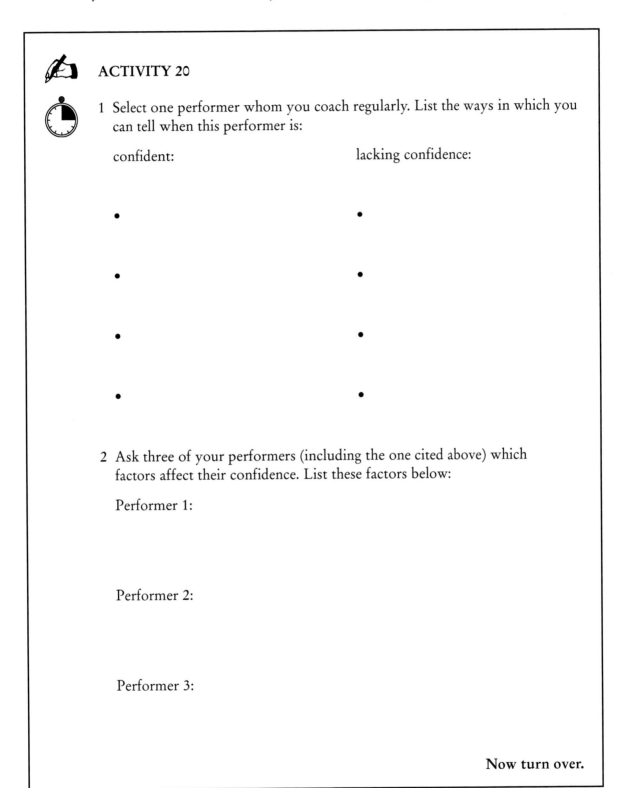

ACTIVITY 20

1 Select one performer whom you coach regularly. List the ways in which you can tell when this performer is:

confident: lacking confidence:

•   •

•   •

•   •

•   •

2 Ask three of your performers (including the one cited above) which factors affect their confidence. List these factors below:

Performer 1:

Performer 2:

Performer 3:

Now turn over.

1 *When performers are confident they tend to:*

- *persevere, even when things are not going well*
- *attempt more challenging tasks and set realistic goals*
- *be positive in their approach*
- *take their share of responsibility for their endeavours (whether they win or lose)*
- *show enthusiasm.*

Less confident performers tend to:

- *give up or lose interest relatively quickly*
- *attempt either easy (to guarantee success) or very difficult tasks (where failure is expected) rather than challenging ones (or set correspondingly inappropriate goals)*
- *think or talk negatively about their participation*
- *either blame others or over-blame themselves for failures*
- *lack enthusiasm for the challenge ahead.*

2 *You may not always have the opportunity to ask performers about their confidence levels (or they may not wish to talk about it). Even if possible, it is unwise to ask performers about confidence immediately before or during competitions or important training sessions. Therefore it is important to recognise when your performers either have or lack confidence. Closely watch some of your other performers in the next training session or competition. Which of the descriptions above applies to them?*

It is important to remember that it is not the situation itself (eg the match, race, training session) that affects self-confidence, but thoughts and expectations about this situation. The diagram below may help to explain this more clearly:

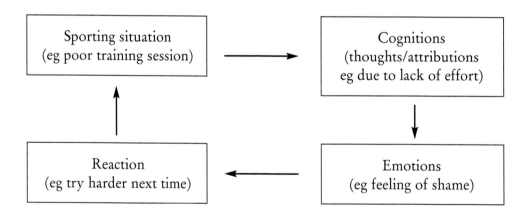

Performers (and coaches) can learn to change the way they think about certain situations, and so change their feelings (eg self-confidence) and other reactions to these situations (eg avoiding the event).

There are a number of ways of improving self-confidence. Mental skills can help performers develop their own self-confidence while your coaching behaviour and communication style[1] can also have positive or negative effects on self-confidence.

Each performer will have or develop preferred techniques for enhancing their self-confidence but some possibilities are given in the following panel.

Situation Facing the Performer	Suggested Technique[2]
Low confidence due to continued poor performance	Goal-setting
Competing against favoured opponents	Imagery
Negative thoughts due to poor form	Positive self-talk
Highly anxious performer who is worried and doubts own ability	Relaxation or redefining what constitutes *success*

If faced by similar situations (to recognise these situations the coach would need to know the performer well), coaches can use a number of approaches to enhance self-confidence. Some are given in the following panel (these examples assume a non-physiological/medical cause for poor form):

Situation Facing the Performer	Suggested Approach
Low confidence due to continued poor performance:	Reduce difficulty of sessions, re-set goals and progressively build back up, ensuring regular success.
Competing against favoured opponents:	Reinforce strengths, reassert personal goals and help develop competition strategy.
Negative thoughts due to poor form:	Help performer use positive self-talk by positive reinforcement.
Highly anxious performer who is worried and doubts own ability:	Help performer reassess goals (and if necessary reduce goal difficulty). Increase positive reinforcements.

---

1   For more information you are recommended to attend the **sports coach UK** workshop **Coaching Methods and Communication.**

2   For a reminder of these techniques, you are referred to Appendix A, page 155.

4.3   Goal-setting to Enhance Self-confidence

Some of the theory of goal-setting described in Chapter Two will be put into practice in the next activity:

ACTIVITY 21

Using a specific performer and the scenarios described in the preceding panels (eg low confidence due to continued poor performance), describe a series of goals to help build his/her self-confidence:

It is essential to identify very clear, specific goals which provide a step-by-step progression for the performer, ensuring regular success. This will first require you to:

- *decide which component of the overall performance is causing difficulty (eg poor last 200m for a 1500m runner, or poor service reception in volleyball)*

- *discuss this with the performer and decide on a realistic goal for this aspect (eg to be able to run last 200m in or under 27 seconds when running at near personal best pace for 1500m, or ensure the receiver is in the optimal receiving position when returning serve)*

- *break down this goal into manageable targets which should be achieved at regular intervals (eg to be able to run 26 seconds for repetitions in a specific training session, run sub-27 seconds for the last 200m in a slowish race and finally, run sub-27 in a fast race, or ensuring early identification of the ball flight, appropriate footwork to get into position, control of the arm position).*

These goals will help the performer focus and direct attention where it is needed. It will also provide a framework in which the performer can assess improvement and feel satisfied when achievement has been reached. *If necessary, go back and modify your goals.*

A problematic issue when setting goals with performers is *goal difficulty.* Each training session should be based on training goals which are challenging but achievable with effort.

 ACTIVITY 22

What percentage of your performers' goals do you expect them to achieve in:

training?   %

competition?   %

Now turn over.

THE LEARNING CENTRE
TOWER HAMLETS COLLEGE
POPLAR CENTRE
POPLAR HIGH STREET
LONDON E14 0AF

Training sessions should provide opportunities for performers to try new techniques and attempt new challenges, but maintain regular success (and so retain self-confidence). The extent to which new techniques are attempted and training success is paramount will depend on the stage of the training/competition cycle. Since training does not usually have the pressure associated with competition (or the significance), training goals can be more difficult than competition goals. For example, a technique which can be performed 70% of the time in training may only be achieved 40% of the time in competition (because of the added pressures associated with competition). Therefore, the goal set for training is often inappropriate for competition (you would probably lose self-confidence if you only had a 40% success rate in competition). While relative failures in training can be used as a learning experiences and provide valuable feedback to help performers improve, in competition such failures can be detrimental to self-confidence. If the coach and performer have set appropriately challenging but realistic goals for competition, the performer should experience success more often than failure.

Repeated failure can result in reduced self-confidence.

ACTIVITY 23

1 In the left-hand column, list some other reasons for low self-confidence:

Reasons	Goals

2 In the right-hand column, describe goals which could help performers
   suffering from low self-confidence.

Now turn over.

Self-confidence is in a constant state of change (over a season, month, week, session). Performers are very sensitive to perceived shifts in fitness, skill level and mental readiness.

Appropriate goal-setting is a way of maintaining progression and protecting against losses in self-confidence.

Use the following example to help you assess your answer. The goals that might be set following a lay-off due to injury might involve the performer aiming to:

- *perform certain sessions/techniques by set dates*

- *adopt a specific training schedule in order to achieve certain fitness targets by a certain date*

- *reach a target weight by a certain date.*

4.4 Implications for Your Coaching

? Think about what you can do to raise or maintain the self-confidence of your performers. Consider:

- your own use of praise and criticism:
  - what language and non-verbal communication[1] do you use when praising and criticising performers?
  - when do you praise and criticise performers and does this depend on whether they have been successful?
  - which (praise or criticism) do you tend to use more and why?
  - how do you change this pattern of feedback when performers are under- or over-confident?
- how you manage each performer's praise and criticism of each other
- how you can help to maintain self-confidence when performers are disappointed
- how you make each performer feel important within the team or group.

In addition to your coaching behaviour, you can also help performers. Learn and use mental skills in training and competition which can help maintain self-confidence. The panels on Page 59 identified important mental skills which must be learned and practised. Sections 4.5 and 4.6 will help you adapt these skills to meet your performers' needs.

---

1 For more information on non-verbal communication (eg body language), you are recommended to attend the **sports coach UK** workshop **Coaching Methods and Communication.** For details of workshops running in your area, visit www.sportscoachuk.org or contact 0113-274 4802.

4.5   Imagery to Enhance Self-confidence

Imagery[1] is a skill you and your performers can use to improve self-confidence. This is the practice of creating a clear mental picture (with the accompanying bodily sensations) of key skills or movement in order to hone or adapt them. For example, a javelin thrower might run through the image of a perfect delivery several times before an actual attempt, including:

- seeing and feeling the withdrawal of the throwing arm, the planting of the front foot and the power of the release

- hearing the javelin in flight and seeing it land perfectly, tip down, close to a personal best distance.

Most top performers use imagery and the examples in the following panel suggest how this can be done.

Use of Imagery

Greg Louganis, 1988 Seoul Olympics diving champion

Louganis visualised himself performing his dives from a number of perspectives (viewpoints) and using several senses (sight, feel, hearing). He viewed these dives from within his own body (as if actually performing the dive), as well as from the pool side (as if he were a coach/judge or watching on video).

Jack Nicklaus, professional golfer

Nicklaus visualises all his shots, using both the sense of sight and feel. He refers to this imagery practice as *going to the movies*. It enables him to play and replay shots over and over again, correcting errors and gaining confidence with each accurate attempt.

---

1   Imagery is sometimes referred to as visualisation, mental rehearsal or mental practice. These are described in more detail in Appendix A, page 155.

Imagery can be a powerful aid to confidence.

ACTIVITY 24

For both training and competition, ask your performers to list the key sensations they experience (you may wish to supplement these with your own experiences as a performer):

Sights in training:

-
-
-

Sights in competition:

-
-
-

Sounds in training:

-
-
-

Sounds in competition:

-
-
-

Smells in training:

-
-
-

Smells in competition:

-
-
-

Bodily (or kinaesthetic) sensations felt in training:

-
-
-

Bodily (or kinaesthetic) sensations felt in competition:

-
-
-

Emotions in training:

-
-
-

Emotions in competition:

-
-
-

Now turn over.

Performers probably recall a range of sensations, the most common of which tend to include the following:

Sight:

- *Opponents*
- *Equipment (eg ball, racket, bat, goal)*
- *Playing area (eg pitch, court, pool, gym, track)*
- *Officials*
- *Spectators*

Sounds:

- *Official's whistle*
- *Voices of opponents, team-mates and spectators*
- *Equipment*
- *Contact sounds (eg ball on bat, spikes on track)*

Smells:

- *Freshly cut grass*
- *Embrocation*
- *Sweat*
- *Newly washed clothing*
- *Leather equipment*

Bodily sensations:

- *Feel of equipment (eg bat in hand)*
- *Body movements*
- *Weather conditions (eg wind in the face, lashing rain)*
- *Contact with opponents*

Emotions:

- *Excitement*
- *Joy*
- *Satisfaction*
- *Frustration*
- *Disappointment*

The greater the number of sensations and the more accurately they are evoked, the greater the benefits from imagery.

Imagery can raise confidence in a number of ways. For example, performers can:

- visualise previous good performances to remind themselves of what success looks and feels like

- imagine various sporting situations and how they will cope with them

- for situations which are new to them, imagine a role-model coping with these new demands

- use imagery to rerun and correct previous problem aspects of performance.

The use of imagery allows the body to become familiar with the sensory response to a particular activity; the muscles and nerves respond in a similar way as when engaged in physical practice. Some performers can visualise more vividly than others but all performers can learn to improve their imagery skills.

 ACTIVITY 25

 1 Select one of your performers and ask him or her to carry out the following (or try it yourself):

- Choose a technique or activity to be practised in the next training session.

- Imagine the training venue: the physical features, the sounds and smells, the feel of the surface underfoot, the equipment to be used and the bodily sensations to be experienced.

- See yourself practising the technique or activity from your own perspective as performer (as if you were actually performing the activity, seeing through your own eyes).

- Now see the same activity as if you were watching yourself (as a coach from the touchline or on video).

- See yourself making a slight error and then see yourself correct the mistake and perform the activity well several times.

- Notice everything about the correct movement(s), the feel, speed, muscle tension, positioning of the limbs, and body's positioning in relation to equipment.

- Recapture the emotions felt when performing the technique or activity.

Continued...

2 Afterwards, ask the performer to answer the following:

- How vividly were you able to see yourself perform?

  Vividly   Not vividly

  1   2   3   4   5

- How well could you feel your body movements?

  Very well   Poorly

  1   2   3   4   5

- How well could you hear the sounds?

  Very well   Poorly

  1   2   3   4   5

- How well did you *experience* the whole activity?

  Very well   Poorly

  1   2   3   4   5

- How aware were you of your emotions/mood?

  Very aware   Not aware

  1   2   3   4   5

This sort of exercise needs to be repeated on a regular basis. With frequent practice, performers will improve their ability to use imagery. If you or your performers want to improve the ability to use imagery effectively, you should work through the sports coach UK mental skills pack on imagery[1]. Once performers have become familiar with imagery techniques, they should be worked into training, and ultimately competition routines.

1   Full references are provided on Page 81.

ACTIVITY 26

1 In the left-hand column, list occasions when performers might use imagery in your sport:

Occasion	Image
eg basketball free shot	eg steady stance, smooth throwing action, angle of release, perfect flight trajectory

2 In the right-hand column, provide a description of what they might image.

Now turn over.

Once your performers are proficient at imagery, they can use it quickly and effectively in a wide variety of situations:

Occasion	Image
During the warm-up	Successful routine, or part of it (eg gymnastics)
Immediately prior to the start of competition	Explosive start (eg athletics/swimming)
During breaks in activity (between points at time-outs)	Correct movement error (eg squash, volleyball)
During change-overs	Next point performed well (eg tennis)
Immediately after performance	Review performance (eg diving)

Look back at your list and at your answers to Activity 2 on page 7. See if you have missed any opportunities for imagery in your sport.

Having identified opportunities to use imagery, you should now provide training sessions which allow performers to use these skills in similar situations.

ACTIVITY 27

For one of your performers, design a training session which incorporates imagery. List the opportunities for imagery (eg during warm-up) and the use you would want performers to make of it in this session:

Opportunities for imagery during session	Use of imagery

Now turn over.

Your session may have included various opportunities to use imagery:

- *An opportunity during the warm-up to image a successful performance.*

- *Each drill or exercise might be preceded by an opportunity to image its successful completion.*

- *Following an error, performers may be allowed to review and correct it.*

- *Following a good performance, performers might be allowed to review and reinforce the correct movements.*

- *During recovery periods following hard physical endeavour.*

- *The session might end with an opportunity for the performer to review the skills and exercises developed in the session, perhaps putting them together into a competitive (imaged) situation.*

You and your performers might find it useful to use a record of imagery (in training and competition) similar to the one in the following panel.

Visualisation Training Record

Session One	**Session Two**
The situation which I plan to visualise is:	The situation which I plan to visualise is:
•	•
The key things to see, hear and feel vividly are:	The key things to see, hear and feel vividly are:
•	•
•	•
•	•
Review: Overall vividness rating (1 = poor, 7 = excellent)	Review: Overall vividness rating (1 = poor, 7 = excellent)
1 2 3 4 5 6 7	1 2 3 4 5 6 7
Things to improve next time:	Things to improve next time:
•	•
•	•

Keep this record and use it to identify any additional opportunities for imagery.

4.6   Positive Self-talk to Enhance Self-confidence

Using positive self-talk is another way of improving confidence. Most people have at some time felt negatively about achieving something and begun to talk themselves out of attaining that particular goal. Injuries, illness and loss of form are all examples of factors that can trigger negative thoughts about performance. Positive self-talk[1] is a way of using positive key words or statements to build self-confidence. Self-talk can help you and performers remain confident at critical moments in your sport. Remember, negative comments you make to performers can also undermine their self-confidence.

ACTIVITY 28

1 Ask performers to review a recent training session or competition and note as accurately as possible the self-statements they made. For each self-statement, they should note the circumstances in which it was made. Two examples are given:

Statement		Circumstances	
I knew I could do that	P	Achieving a new technique	W
I can't play in this weather	N	Poor weather conditions	B
•		•	
•		•	
•		•	

2 Read the following and place the appropriate letters in the boxes provided after each statement circumstance:

- Was the self-statement positive (P) or negative (N)?
- Was the participant performing well (W) or badly (B) at the time?

Continued...

---

1   Or more accurately **affirmation self-talk** (there are various types of self-talk).

3 Describe any pattern that seems to be occurring:

*Performers (and coaches) are often perfectionists by nature and therefore tend to indulge in self-criticism (negative self-talk). You can help performers counter this and create positive images of themselves by encouraging **affirmation statements** – statements that reflect positive attitudes or thoughts about oneself. These affirmations are most effective when they are believable and vivid.*

You might suggest that performers keep a self-talk log, which could be completed after each session or competition. This would elicit the sort of information that was requested in the last activity. Performers (and coaches) can use this information to identify the occurrence of negative self-talk and develop a strategy for using affirmation statements.

In the following panel you will find an example page from a self-talk log:

Session/competition:	Self-statements
Circuit training session:	'Can't keep this up for three sets' *(negative)*.
	'Oh no, the rope climb next' *(negative)*.
	'That wasn't too bad, next set I'll really go for it' *(positive)*.
Volleyball tournament:	'We're just going to work hard as a team and the results will come' *(positive)*.
	'We'll never beat this team' *(negative)*.
	'I just can't get it past that guy' *(negative)*.
	'I know we have the skills to beat this team' *(positive)*.

There can be problems with keeping this kind of log, such as:

- remembering self-statements
- recalling the circumstances that prompted self-statements
- having time to complete the log straight after an event.

All of these difficulties can be reduced with practice. Keeping the log close at hand so that as little time as possible elapses between making and recording self-statements will also help.

  ACTIVITY 29

1 Ask your performers to keep a self-talk log, noting the self-statements they make during (or after) training and competition.

2 Note here any difficulties performers have completing a self-talk log:

- •   •

- •   •

This information can be used to build up a picture of how performers view themselves and their sporting efforts. It also helps identify any pattern of self-critical comments performers develop which coaches can then address.

The first stage in altering negative thoughts is to stop them when they occur. The performer needs to recognise a negative thought and stop it using a trigger word (eg stop, halt, change) or action (eg leg slap, finger snap). This should initially be done in training rather than in competition.

*I **can** do it.*

ACTIVITY 30

1 Ask one or two performers to turn the following negative statements into positive ones (you might try this yourself). Encourage them to add one or two of their own:

Negative self-talk: Positive self-talk:

- I always perform poorly against that opponent.

- These conditions don't suit me.

- No one in the team seems to be playing well.

- I don't want to lose.

2 Ask the same performers to imagine a situation in their sport in which they often have negative thoughts (eg before tossing ball up on serve in tennis, while moving in to tackle in rugby, following a slow first lap in a race, during a poor training session). They should then **briefly** recall the negative statements they usually make. Once they have recreated this situation in their minds, ask them to interrupt these thoughts using the trigger word or action of their choice. They can then use positive self-talk to develop more self-confidence.

Now turn over.

1   *Performers should learn to change any negative self-talk into positive as soon as they recognise it. This will come with practice but the following provides some examples:*

Negative self-talk:	*Positive self-talk:*
• *I always perform poorly against that opponent.*	• *She'll expect to beat me so I will surprise her.*
• *These conditions don't suit me.*	• *Nobody likes this weather; I can play as well as anyone.*
• *No one in the team seems to be playing well.*	• *We can all help each other to improve.*
• *I don't want to lose.*	• *As long as I give my best, I'll always be successful.*

2   *This recreation of negative thoughts and subsequent stopping using trigger words should be repeated until it becomes automatic. Performers should reach the stage where each time they have a negative thought about their performance, they immediately stop it using the trigger word. This will take plenty of practise (old bad habits take time to change).*

Once negative thoughts have been stopped, they should be replaced immediately by positive ones[1].

Negative self-talk and thoughts can occur after the event. Poor or unexpected results often trigger complex explanations about why the outcome occurred. At this often emotive time, performers sometimes focus on factors which lie outside their control (eg poor conditions, bad luck, better opponents). The danger is that these performers can then see no way of improving when faced with similar situations in the future. When evaluating a performance (often best left until the initial emotional reaction is passed), you should help your performers focus on positive aspects of performance and those factors over which they and you have some control (eg skills, effort, fitness, tactics). The use of positive self-statements and the techniques described in this chapter can be of great help at this time.

Self-confidence will enable performers to attempt new challenges, recover quickly from disappointments and enjoy their sports involvement, regardless of the result. The techniques described in this section will help you develop self-confidence in your performers (the same techniques will work for you as a coach).

The preceding mental skills can be used by performers to enhance and maintain self-confidence. The following Action Plan will help integrate these skills into your coaching sessions. However, remember that your coaching behaviour and communication style can also affect a performer's self-confidence.

---

1   Cognitive restructuring is dealt with in more detail in the **sports coach UK** workshop **Motivation and Mental Toughness**. For further details contact **sports coach UK** on 0113-274 4802. For details of workshops running in your area, contact your home country's office or visit www.sportscoachuk.org

4.7   Recap and What Next?

This chapter has examined the importance of self-confidence on sports performance. You have assessed the self-confidence of your performers and examined ways in which it can be enhanced. Finally, you have identified practical examples of how your performers can use these techniques to improve their self-confidence.

Action Plan

Use the action plan in Chapter Two (page 34) to identify performers with low self-confidence. Selecting one example, design a practical strategy to enhance this performer's self-confidence. Detail how your training schedule and coaching practice would develop self-confidence, including an example of a coaching session designed to build confidence. Implement this strategy, monitor its progress and evaluate its success.

The following will complement information given in this chapter:

sports coach UK (1999) **Motivation and Mental Toughness.**
Leeds, **sports coach UK**. ISBN 0 902523 24 5.

The following are suggested for those wishing to develop a greater understanding of topics presented in this chapter:

Bunker, L and Williams, JM (1986) **Cognitive techniques for improving performance and building confidence.**
<u>In</u> Williams, JM (1986) Applied sport psychology: personal growth to peak performance.
Palo Alto, CA, Mayfield. ISBN 0 76741 747 X.

The following **sports coach UK** workshops may be useful:

Motivation and Mental Toughness

Goal-setting and Planning

Performance Profiling

For details of workshops running in your area, visit www.sportscoachuk.org or contact 0113-274 4802.

CHAPTER FIVE

Concentration

Chapter Five: Concentration

5.0 What's in It for You?

Most coaches and performers recognise that the ability to concentrate is a prerequisite for effective performance. Performers may have to switch their attention to many things during the course of a training session or competition. Performers differ in their ability to do this and in the way they cope with distractions.

There are a number of simple routines or tasks you can build into your normal coaching practices which can be used in competition to improve a performer's ability to concentrate. In this chapter, you will be given the opportunity to look at some possibilities and develop some ideas to help your own performers. By the end of this chapter, you should be able to:

- describe what is meant by concentration
- explain how concentration affects performance in your sport
- identify the need for different ways of focusing attention in your sport
- identify appropriate components of performance on which to focus attention
- identify the key distractions which affect your performers
- evaluate the ability of your performers to maintain concentration
- identify strategies to develop concentration in training and competition
- design an action plan to improve a performer's concentration.

5.1 Importance of Concentration

How often have you heard the following comments from performers in your sport?

- 'I just couldn't concentrate'
- 'I'm just going to focus on my game and ignore the opposition'
- 'I'm only going to think about one aspect at a time'
- 'I didn't even notice the crowd'

How often have you (or other coaches) shouted the words *concentrate* or *focus*? All of these phrases relate to concentration. This is the mental quality of keeping your mind on the *here and now* and focusing on aspects of performance essential for success. Without concentration, all the performer's skills and fitness acquired in training will be at best unfocused and at worst wasted. However shouting the word *concentrate* does not help the performer focus on important aspects of performance.

Focus on the here and now.

ACTIVITY 31

For a fundamental skill in your sport (preferably one you have worked on recently with performers), list two or three key components on which the performer should focus:

•

•

•

Now turn over.

The examples given below suggest components on which tennis and judo players might focus:

Tennis approach shot:

Novice:

* *Footwork and balance*
* *Angle of the racket*
* *Correct body position*
* *Contact of ball and racket*
* *Follow through*
* *Creating space*

Experienced performer:

* *Position of opponent*
* *Trajectory and spin of the ball*
* *Available space to use*
* *Position after the shot*

Judo throw:

Novice:

* *Hold on opponent*
* *Footwork*
* *Own balance*
* *Speed of body movement*

Experienced performer:

* *Moving into suitable position*
* *Opponent's balance*
* *Avoiding counter-attack*
* *Identifying precise moment of attack*

You will notice that some of these aspects of performance (cues) are internal to the performer (eg body position), while others relate to external factors (eg opponent's ball, environment). Experienced performers are able to identify the critical cues early in the event (eg the position of the bowler's hand before a delivery) and so anticipate what to expect (eg a short, fast delivery). This enables them to take appropriate action (eg get into position for a hook shot or duck below the ball). Coaches can help novice performers identify and focus on these critical cues.

As coach, you must help performers focus on cues appropriate to their level of skill development. For example, the novice performer would probably focus on elementary aspects of the opponent's movements or the environment (eg the terrain), whereas more experienced performers would look for subtle differences in opponents' actions or try to anticipate less immediate behaviour (eg not only the opponent's next shot, but the one after that). Where performers find it difficult to focus on appropriate cues, you should create a training environment which makes this easier (eg for the novice, breaking a technique down into its components and identifying where to focus.

In order to focus on these (or any other) components of performance, each individual must develop concentration. If performers are unable to concentrate or are distracted, the skill will either not be mastered or may break down under competitive pressure.

Performers can focus on various objects within the sporting contest, for example:

- the opponent
- their own bodily sensations and position
- their team-mates
- the equipment (eg the ball, bow, hurdle)
- the environment.

ACTIVITY 32

Ask performers what they typically focus on when performing certain drills or practices in training:

Type of drill/practice: Focus:

-   -

                                                     -

-   -

                                                     -

-   -

                                                     -

-   -

                                                     -

Now turn over.

The research identifies a number of different types of attentional focus. The broad-narrow continuum defines the extent to which the performer focuses on a large or small number of stimuli (eg broad – opposing team players' movements; narrow – grip on the racket). The internal-external continuum specifies whether the focus is on stimuli internal to the performer (eg feelings of fatigue) or external (eg officials, ball). The following diagram illustrates this by categorising examples of the sorts of things on which performers tend to focus:

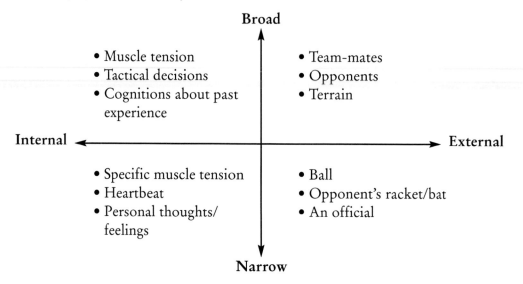

Attentional style (the extent to which a performer uses a broad or narrow, internal or external focus) should depend on the demands of the sport, but often is influenced by individual preferences of style. For example:

- In open play in soccer, the player would need an external and broad focus of attention (to identify the moves of team-mates and opponents). This might shift to a narrow external focus when controlling the ball or taking a penalty.

- The weightlifter would probably have an external and narrow focus when approaching the bar and taking the correct position, and an internal and narrow focus when attending to bodily sensations and personal readiness to lift.

Effective performers will vary their attentional style to meet their changing needs.

I channel my concentration into just the few seconds before each ball is bowled. Then I switch off, and perhaps have a laugh or a joke with the other slips and the wicketkeeper, or even the batsman. It helps me and my mates because it keeps them relaxed, and so they don't get tired or bored so easily if we're having a hard time of it.

Ian Botham, Cricket My Way, 1989 (p 159)

ACTIVITY 33

1 Following the next competition, ask your performers to note down the key things on which they concentrated during the event (left-hand column):

Focus	Attentional style

2 In the right-hand column, categorise each focal point according to the attentional style required (eg goal-keeper during a penalty, external-narrow).

3 Ask performers:

- how their focus changes during competition:

- for how long they focus on each of these objects:

- where their focus typically goes when they are distracted:

4 Place the demands of your sport on the concentration continuum:

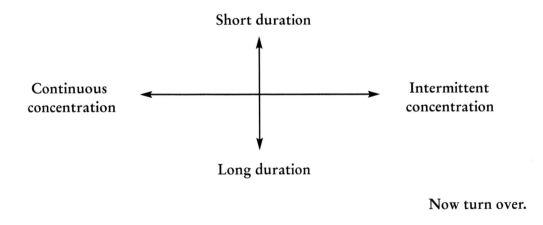

Now turn over.

1/2 *Performers concentrate in their own unique way. The focus of attention may also shift during a competition or training session. For example, the focus might be:*

- *the outstanding opponent (during the first quarter of a match) – external/narrow*
- *the referee (once a player has been booked) – external/narrow*
- *the barriers (towards the end of a steeplechase) – external/narrow*
- *a particular skill or manoeuvre (following several mistakes) – internal/broad or narrow*
- *the opposing team's play (when trying to break down a defence) – external/broad*
- *the performer's own body sensations (eg when fatigued or injured) – internal/broad or narrow.*

3 *Sports vary in the concentration demands they place on the performer. Sports requiring sustained concentration over relatively long periods of time include:*

- *tennis, squash, badminton, hockey – some players switch in and out of concentration, others concentrate throughout*
- *road cycling, distance running – concentration must be maintained throughout.*

Other sports place short-burst concentration demands (over an extended period) on performers, for example, cricket, golf, shooting events and athletics (field events).

Some sports require intense concentration for a relatively short period such as slalom canoeing, sprinting events (swimming, athletics), bobsleigh and alpine skiing.

What happens to concentration when a performer is distracted is considered in more detail in the next section. Typically it appears to move away from the here and now – back to dwell on what has happened (eg a mistake) or ahead to what might happen (eg the result). It might focus internally (eg on personal thoughts and fears) or externally (eg onto a specific source of distraction such as the weather).

4 *The examples provided in the following diagram might help you locate your sport on the concentration continuum:*

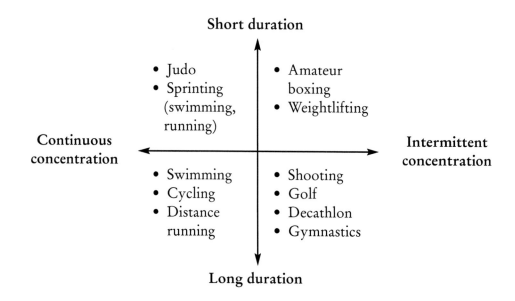

Look back at your profiles in Chapter Two (page 34) and examine the perceived need to concentrate.

5.2   Distractions

Unfortunately, concentration is easily broken, as you will have been reminded in the last activity. In sport, as in all areas of life, potential distractions are everywhere resulting in performers no longer remaining in the here and now.

  ACTIVITY 34

List the main distractions in your sport. For each one, comment on the effect it might have on performance:

Distraction	Effect on performance

Now turn over.

Common distractions in sport include:

- *mistakes/errors*
- *anxiety*
- *opponents*
- *other performers (not opponents)*
- *decisions of officials*
- *spectators*
- *irrelevant thoughts (sporting or non-sporting)*
- *fatigue*
- *music (eg gymnastics)*
- *the weather or conditions underfoot*
- *public announcements*
- *the coach or important others.*

Effects vary from a general loss in concentration to increased anxiety and decreased self-confidence (which can themselves be potential distractions). The exact effect will depend on the nature of the sport.

Sports performers are bombarded with information from various sources (all the above plus the sport relevant information such as from the opposition, team-mates, officials and equipment). This information can be internal – from within the performer (eg anxiety) or external – factors outside of the performer (eg official's decisions). However, people can only attend to a limited amount of information at any one time (a so-called limited capacity[1]). Distractions provide irrelevant information which reduces the ability of the performer to deal with the relevant demands of the task, session or competition (eg worrying about the outcome reduces the capacity to concentrate on the activity, skill or movement at hand). As a result of losing concentration, performers miss important information (cues) or make poor decisions. Increasing the ability to focus on relevant information and switch off distractions will promote improved learning and more consistent performance.

 When coaching a new technique (and especially with inexperienced performers), you must provide a coaching environment which reduces irrelevant and distracting information.

1   Information processing is covered in detail in the **sports coach UK** workshop **Improving Practices and Skill.** For further details contact **sports coach UK** on 0113-274 4802. For details of workshops running in your area, visit www.sportscoachuk.org or contact 0113-274 4802.

ACTIVITY 35

How can you tell if your performers are having difficulty concentrating? List the things you notice (eg being slow to respond to the movements or actions of team-mates):

-
-
-
-
-
-

Now turn over.

There are various symptoms which could be attributed to poor concentration. For example:

- *not keeping up with the action*
- *showing signs of anger or frustration*
- *missing key opportunities (eg to pass, shoot, attack)*
- *making poor decisions*
- *timing errors (eg fumbling the ball, missing checkmarks, mistiming the shot)*
- *attending to irrelevant information (eg spectators).*

? In the next competition or training session, watch your performers for signs of poor concentration.

You will probably find that some performers are better able to concentrate than others and some are more easily distracted than others. For each performer who suffers from poor concentration, you will need to devise a concentration training programme which will enhance this quality and ultimately improve performance.

5.3   Strategies for Improving Concentration

Strategies for improving concentration are often very personal in nature. Performers develop their own routines and habits which they tend to repeat before and during every event. There are various concentration techniques which have proved valuable in sport and which can be built into these performance routines.

One of the ways to maintain focus is to set process goals for each session or competition[1]. For any training session or competition, the performer will have an overall (product) goal. To achieve this goal, the performer will devise a number of process (or action) goals which help focus on specific aspects of the task. For each one of these goals, performers can use a **trigger word**, a word which associates with the goal and instantly reminds them of the objective. These trigger words can be:

- instructional (eg follow through, quick release, look up, smooth)
- motivational (eg make it big, attack).

Trigger words can also help the performer concentrate on the here and now (ie not worry or think about a previous or future point or play). Read the example in the following panel and then try the next activity.

---

1   If you are unsure about goal-setting, look back at page 29 or refer to **sports coach UK**'s resource **Coaching Sessions: A Guide to Planning and Goal-setting**. Available from **Coachwise 1st4sport** (tel: 0113-201 5555 or visit www.1st4sport.com).

Badminton Player Example

Process goals: Trigger words:

- 80% of service returns to the back of the court.   - Long

- Try to keep on my toes, especially towards end of match.   - Bounce

- Keep opponent moving around the court.   - Stretch

- Stick to pre-game plan.   - Think

  ACTIVITY 36

1 For one of your next coaching sessions or competitions, devise with your performer a number of process goals which will help achieve the product goal. List these in the left-hand column:

Process Goals	Trigger Words
a	
b	
c	
d	

2 Ask the performer to assign a trigger word for each process goal. This should instantly remind the performer of the goal to be achieved. These should be listed in the right-hand column. The performer should then use these goals and trigger words within the event.

3 Following this event, ask the performer to score his or her ability to concentrate on these goals (using the scale below):

Goal a: Easy to concentrate   ← 1 2 3 4 5 →   Difficult to concentrate

Goal b: Easy to concentrate   ← 1 2 3 4 5 →   Difficult to concentrate

Goal c: Easy to concentrate   ← 1 2 3 4 5 →   Difficult to concentrate

Goal d: Easy to concentrate   ← 1 2 3 4 5 →   Difficult to concentrate

You will probably find that some performers are better able to concentrate on certain aspects of performance than others. This is only natural. You will need to use some of the following techniques to help those who find concentration difficult.

Goals for each training session and competition are only effective if they are remembered by performers. While this may seem obvious, it is something with which performers often have difficulty, especially under the pressure of important competitions.

One way of helping performers remember their goals is to encourage them to prepare **crib cards**, written reminders which can be put in everyday places (eg bathroom mirror, fridge door) to jog their memories. These cards should be concise, contain key words or phrases (no more than three or four) and depict aspects of competition on which to focus or feelings performers might experience.

An example of a crib card used by a javelin thrower is given in the panel below.

Remember:

- *Deep breath and focus.*
- *Controlled run up.*
- *Fast strike (BANG).*

These short phrases help the thrower keep each attempt simple and consistent. The emotive *BANG* should trigger an explosive release. This crib card was kept on the thrower's drinking bottle (which was used before each attempt).

 As coach, you may develop your own crib cards to help you concentrate on key aspects of your coaching (eg use of non-verbal communication, giving clear demonstration).

ACTIVITY 37

Help one of your performers create a crib card for his or her next competition. Write the key phrases below and explain their intended effects:

Key words: Intended effect:

•

•

•

•

•

•

Now turn over.

Each word or phrase should generate desired behaviour in a particular order and be directed at achieving a key objective. They should be simple to understand and remember. This crib card should be placed somewhere so the performer sees it frequently and especially immediately before competition (eg in the performer's kit bag, stuck to a drinks bottle or placed in the performer's competition shoes or boots). Alternatively, they can be placed on audiotape (along with positive self-statements) which the performer can play during the warm-up, between attempts (eg javelin throws) or even at half-time (eg soccer, hockey).

Segmenting

In your sport there may be natural breaks in performance which enable you to divide it into **segments**. These segments can be divided by time, breaks in the action or scores. Having a goal for each segment will help your performer keep concentrating throughout the event.

ACTIVITY 38

1 Read the following examples and then divide your sport into logical segments (describing the start and finish of each one in the left hand column):

Segment	Goal/Concentrate on
First lap (athletics)	*Get into a rhythm and stay close to the leader.*
Line out (rugby)	*Clear instructions, straight throw.*
Approach to vault (gymnastics)	*Controlled speed on approach.*

2 In the right-hand column, devise a process goal for your performer to concentrate on during each segment.

How you segment your sport and the type of goals you set will depend on the nature of the sport and the preferences of the performer. Segments should seem logical and clear to performers, enabling them to divide their overall competition plan into manageable chunks. Check your answers again.

Routines

Most sports performers will develop some form of routine for competition days. This may include specific activities on the night before, the morning of the competition, during warm-ups, competition and post-competition routines. Performers may also have specific routines before individual techniques (eg the kicker in rugby may take a set number of steps backward, focus on the posts, take a deep breath, imagine the ball passing through the posts, say a trigger word to relax before taking the kick). If these routines are appropriately structured, they can prove a useful aid to concentration.

Routines can aid concentration.

During the period leading up to competition, performers will undertake a physical warm-up. This allows the body to prepare for the physical and psychological demands ahead. This time is also valuable for focusing attention on the key objectives (goals). Therefore, performers should remind themselves of their process goals during their warm-up/pre-event routine.

This time also provides an opportunity to utilise imagery skills. Performers can visualise themselves successfully performing and achieving each of their process goals, feeling themselves successfully completing the task (in the badminton example on page 97, this would mean visualising themselves returning 80% of serves, achieving good positioning, moving their opponent around the court and sticking to their game plan).

ACTIVITY 39

During the warm-up for the next training session or competition, ask your performers to recall their process goals (accompanied by positive affirmation statements) and then visualise themselves achieving these goals[1]. Ask them how well they managed to do this and summarise any comments made:

Performers should find that as they repeat these successful performances, their confidence in their ability to achieve these goals grows. The more skilled they become at imagery, the more easily they will be able to visualise a successful performance and identify the factors that contribute to it.

As important as focusing attention before the start of a competition is the ability to focus and refocus during an event. There will be numerous occasions within a competition when performers will need to block out distractions and concentrate on a specific skill or aspect of performance ahead. This is especially the case with closed skills[2].

---

1   It is important that this pre-training (and similarly pre-competition) visualisation is of successful performances, since visualising unsuccessful performance may be detrimental to self-confidence.

2   A closed skill is one where there is a discrete beginning and end, is largely independent on external factors (eg other performers or opponents), and begins at the performer's will (eg a golf drive, basketball free throw, long-jump run up).

ACTIVITY 40

With your performers, identify opportunities in competition when performance routines can be used and devise routines which can be carried out prior to each specified segment:

Segment	Routine

Each sports event will have its own framework and timescales. However, all sports provide opportunities for competition routines. Some are provided in the following panel.

Opportunities for Routine Within Competition:

Football:	*Penalty kick/free kick/throw in/goal kick*
Rugby:	*Line-out/scrum/drop-out/penalty kick*
Racket sports:	*Between points/between games*
Cricket:	*Between deliveries/overs*
Athletics (throws and jumps):	*On the runway/between attempts*
Basketball:	*Free throw line*
Target sports:	*Between attempts*

To highlight the use of a performance routine, the following tennis example is provided. As you read through the routine, consider the parallels with your own sport.

Tennis Serve

- *Decide on the service type and make the appropriate technical adjustments.*

- *Take a deep breath: before serving, a breath should be taken to help you relax and focus.*

- *Bounce the ball: bouncing the ball should help you gain rhythm – this should be repeated as many times as necessary.*

- *Visualise a good serve: just before serving, visualise the sight and feel of a good serve, delivered to the exact spot at which you are aiming, seeing the ball follow a predetermined trajectory.*

- *Serve, concentrating on one or two key aspects (eg follow through).*

Performers using such a routine should first try it, evaluate its effectiveness and then adjust it if necessary. Performers should go through their routine each time they are preparing to serve.

Each segment of the competition should now have a specific process goal and each closed skill a performance routine to follow. Each performer should utilise these routines according to their own strengths, weaknesses and needs. *If necessary, go back and revise or extend your answer to the last activity.*

Competition (Distraction) Training

As performers become more skilled at focusing on the key objectives in training (using process goals, trigger words, routines and imagery), you may wish to simulate competition conditions in training. This will allow the performer to develop concentration in a controlled atmosphere which contains some of the competition distractions.

Study the following panel which provides examples of a distraction training session[1] and then try the next activity.

Football

This practice requires two/three players.

Player One has 20–30 balls which are passed one at a time to Player Two at regular intervals (about five seconds). As the ball is passed, Player One calls left or right respectively. Player Two has to pass the ball to a cone (or other marker) placed to the left or right according to what is called by Player One. The distances between players, Player Two and cones, and the speed of passing can be manipulated to alter difficulty. Once Player One can do this effectively, background noises can be added (eg on tape) or a third person can run between the cones to act as a visual distraction.

Tennis

This practice requires one player and a feeder machine (or two players if no machine is available).

The player stands close to the net in a volleying position. The feeder machine (or Player Two) feeds balls at ever increasing frequency. The player should aim to punch the volley away (preferably to a designated spot). As the balls arrive more frequently, the player should aim to remain relaxed and concentrate only on body position and the next shot. Once competent, the player is instructed to take one or two steps left or right between volleys, returning to the ideal volleying position as soon as possible. This movement acts as a physical distraction.

---

1   For help with learning concentration skills, you are referred to the **sports coach UK** resource **Improving Concentration**. Available from **Coachwise 1st4sport** (tel: 0113-201 5555 or visit www.1st4sport.com).

Distance Running

This exercise improves pace-judgement. For this activity, the runner must wear a suitable portable tape recorder with headphones.

The runner is instructed to run around a circuit (athletics track, road or grass circuit) at a constant pace (wearing the tape recorder). Once the runner has achieved a constant pace, the tape recorder should be turned on. This should play either music which the runner finds inspirational (eg the theme from *Chariots of Fire*) or some other form of distraction (eg a voice giving distracting information or crowd noise). The runner should check lap times and aim to maintain an even pace throughout.

Music should be inspirational.

ACTIVITY 41

Look back at your list of competition distractions on page 93. Devise a training session in which these distractions could be simulated (you may wish to focus on one distraction or a number of distractions during the session):

Distraction	Description of Simulation

Now turn over.

By the end of any programme designed to simulate competition distractions, the performer should be performing under conditions as similar to competition as possible. The following examples might provide you with some ideas. Read through them and add any new ideas to your session:

Distraction	*Description of Simulation*
Crowd noise	*Use of pre-recorded tape containing progressively distracting crowd noises.*
Unfavourable official's decisions	*Coach plays official's role and incorporates unfavourable decisions.*
Aggressive opponent	*Team-mate plays aggressive (but non-violent) opponent and attempts to provoke response.*
Fatigue	*Performer alternates between sport specific exercise of increasing intensity (to induce fatigue) and skills exercises.*

5.4   Implications for Your Coaching

The ability of performers to concentrate on those cues most critical to their event can be enhanced by helping them develop concentration skills. These skills will only be beneficial if performers know on what to concentrate, how to distinguish those cues from the mass of information they receive, and remain focused when distractions occur. It also requires the coach not to provide irrelevant or too much information which can act as distractions.

Action Plan
Use the action plan in Chapter Two (page 34) to identify situations where the ability of a performer to concentrate is poor. Selecting one example, design a practical strategy to enhance this performer's concentration, including an outline of a coaching session designed to develop concentration. This should include how you will structure the session to help this performer identify and focus on critical information cues. Detail the techniques you would use. Implement this strategy, monitor its progress and evaluate its success.

5.5   Recap and What Next?

This chapter has explored the concentration requirements of your sport. You will have observed your performers in action and identified their ability to concentrate in sporting situations. You will have noted the key distractions that they face. Various techniques for developing concentration have been introduced and you have had an opportunity to apply them to your own coaching situations.

The following **sports coach UK** workshops may be useful:

Motivation and Mental Toughness

Imagery Training and **Performance Profiling**.

For details of workshops running in your area, visit www.sportscoachuk.org or contact 0113-274 4802.

CHAPTER SIX

Emotional Control

Chapter Six: Emotional Control

6.0 What's in It for You?

Taking part in sport is by its very nature emotional: the joy of success, the disappointment of failure, the fear of injury, the determination to achieve, the pride in performance. These and many more emotions pervade sport at all levels of participation.

Emotions can be negative or positive and a performer's (and coach's) ability to cope with these feelings and remain positive in the face of adversity is essential to successful performance. This chapter will explore emotional control. By the end of this chapter, you should be able to:

- describe emotional control
- describe situations where your performers lose emotional control
- explain how emotional control affects performance in your sport
- evaluate the emotional control of performers in various sporting situations
- identify strategies to develop emotional control
- identify ways in which your behaviour can effect a performer's emotional control
- design an action plan to develop a performer's emotional control.

Performers should at all times maintain emotional control.

6.1 Explaining Emotions

Identifying when your performers feel particular emotions and understanding the reason for these feelings is the first part of helping performers gain emotional control.

Negative and positive emotions.

ACTIVITY 42

List the positive and negative emotions that may be felt in your sport and give
an example of the situations in which they occur:

Positive emotion: Situation:

•   •

•   •

•   •

Negative emotion: Situation:

•   •

•   •

•   •

Now turn over.

Some of the most commonly felt emotions in sport include:

Positive emotions:	*Negative emotions:*
• *Joy*	• *Sadness*
• *Excitement*	• *Anger*
• *Determination*	• *Aggression*
• *Pride*	• *Lethargy*
• *Assertiveness*	• *Reluctance*
• *Confidence*	• *Self-doubt*
• *Calmness*	• *Fear*
• *Satisfaction*	• *Frustration*

Emotions are influenced by factors both within and outside the sport. The way in which performers explain what has happened (or what they expect to happen) to them will influence their feelings towards these events. It is, therefore, not so much the outcome (eg good training session, bad competition, occurrence of an injury) that determines the emotions felt, as the explanation of why it happened. The effects on performers of a given emotion can also vary. For example, anxiety can be either facilitative (help performers) or debilitative, depending on the perceptions of the performer. By helping performers explain events in a positive and constructive way, you will help to increase positive feelings and minimise the potential negative effects of emotions.

Feeling strong emotions before, during or after a competition is perfectly natural. What is important is the ability to control these feelings so they do not undermine performance. Two emotions which are often associated with poor performance are:

• anxiety

• anger.

6.2   Anxiety: the Performer's Curse

Many people consider anxiety to be the reverse side of self-confidence. Although not strictly the case, it is true that when confident, performers are often less anxious and when performers become anxious, their self-confidence often drops. Performers become anxious when they perceive they cannot meet the demands of the next session, competition or season. This is more likely to occur when self-confidence is low. Performers are not the only ones who can become anxious, coaches can too.

Anxiety is distinct from other terms with which it is often confused:

• Arousal – a general physiological state which when heightened can be either pleasant (excitement) or unpleasant (fright).

• Stress – the reaction experienced in response to the stresses of a task which lies ahead, which can either be positive or negative.

Commonly, anxiety is related to feelings of tension, lethargy and worry, and as such is to be reduced whenever possible. However, some performers are able to cope with anxiety and actually use it to facilitate performance.

ACTIVITY 43

1   What symptoms of anxiety do your performers display? List and categorise
    them in a way which seems appropriate:

Symptom	Category

2   What effects does anxiety have on your performers?

   •

   •

   •

   •

3   What anxiety symptoms do you (the coach) experience or show?

   •

   •

Now turn over.

1   *Anxiety tends to be categorised according to the symptoms that accompany it. These tend to be categorised into physical (bodily or **somatic**) and mental (**cognitive**) anxiety:*

Category	Symptom
Bodily (somatic) anxiety	Butterflies Sweaty hands Needing the toilet Muscle tension Raised heart rate Nausea
Mental (cognitive) anxiety	Worry Negative thoughts Self-criticism Confusion Lack of attention

Go back to your list and place the letter S next to those symptoms which are somatic and a C next to those which are cognitive.

2/3 *These symptoms affect performers in different ways but the consequences are often detrimental. Somatic symptoms can become a distraction to performers (who may worry about the physical sensations they are experiencing) or can cause the skill execution to break down (eg sweaty, shaky hands causing a poor shot or catch). Cognitive symptoms are also a distraction, limiting the capacity to concentrate on the key aspects of the sport. They may also undermine self-confidence, resulting as they often do from a focus on the outcome rather than the task at hand (eg a performer worrying about losing the match, consequently not being selected for a representative squad and losing the expected peer respect, rather than focusing on what is needed to be successful).*

Many factors can contribute to the development of anxiety. Some of these may be personal to the performer (eg a fear of failure, unrealistic personal goals), while others may be due to pressures imposed by others (eg the coach's high expectations, excessive media attention, peer pressure to excel).

 It is therefore essential that you watch out for signs of anxiety in your performers and consider all the possible causes (including your own behaviour in training and on competition days). It is only then that you can take appropriate action.

The techniques which can be used to reduce anxiety (collectively called **relaxation skills**) fall into two broad categories:

- Body-to-mind (where the body is relaxed, with the assumption that this will lead to a reduction in negative thoughts).

- Mind-to-body (where the mind is relaxed, with the assumption that this will lead to a reduction in physical tension).

The benefits of relaxation are numerous but primarily allow performers to reduce muscular tension and worrying thoughts. As a result they are able to concentrate their minds on the sporting situations they face and effectively execute the movements required. These relaxation techniques are often practised before other mental skills are undertaken (ie goal-setting, imagery, concentration skills are often more effectively performed when the performer is relaxed)[1].

---

1   For more information and practical exercises in relaxation, try the **sports coach UK** resource **Handling Pressure**. Available from **Coachwise 1st4sport** (tel: 0113-201 5555 or visit www.1st4sport.com).

Many of the symptoms described previously are not directly visible to the coach's eye. How do you know when your performers are anxious? Try the next activity.

ACTIVITY 44

1 Select three of your performers and write in the left-hand column what you notice when each is anxious:

	Your Observations	Performer's Observations
Example:	They talk a lot.	I forget what I should be doing.
Performer 1		
Performer 2		
Performer 3		

2 Now ask these performers what they notice when they are anxious. Summarise their answers in the right-hand column.

You probably found that each performer behaves differently when anxious. Some display their nerves and appear anxious, some seem quiet, some yawn, while others become boisterous. It is only by knowing your performers that an accurate recognition of their feelings can be made so that a genuine assessment of their needs can be undertaken.

Performers can use a log or diary to record their feelings of anxiety before and during each training session and competition. Once the coach and performer recognise the signs of anxiety, they can start to work on reducing it.

 Do you become anxious on the day of competition? You need to be aware of your own behaviour and its effect on performers.

6.3 Managing Anxiety

Recognising anxiety is only part of the strategy. The next step is to manage it. One of the most commonly used relaxation techniques is that of **Progressive Muscular Relaxation (PMR)**. This is a body-to-mind technique which encourages the performer to alternate tensing and relaxing the body's muscles, moving around the body from head and neck to lower legs and feet[1]. Try the next activity with performers from your sport[2].

  ACTIVITY 45

 Following a training session, ask performers to note down the main muscle groups they have used in the session (or a specific technique or routine in their sport). Suggest that they use simple names (eg thighs, calves, forearm). Focusing on these muscle groups, ask each performer to tense and then relax each muscle in turn. Use the following sequence for each muscle group:

- Tense the muscles for about five seconds (stop any muscle contraction if pain is experienced).

- When the muscles are contracted, notice the sensation of tension.

- Now completely relax the muscles.

- Notice the difference between relaxed and tense muscles.

- Repeat two or three times.

This technique is useful the night before competition to help performers relax and sleep.

---

1   PMR is described in detail in **sports coach UK**'s resource **Handling Pressure**.
2   This should initially be performed before training rather than competition.

To check a performer's progress in using this technique, you may wish to use a relaxation record log:

Relaxation Training Record							
Training Session:	Tense Fairly relaxed Very relaxed 1 ←——————————————→ 7 (Circle as appropriate)						
Day One Comments:	1	2	3	4	5	6	7
Day Two Comments:	1	2	3	4	5	6	7
Day Three Comments:	1	2	3	4	5	6	7
Day Four Comments:	1	2	3	4	5	6	7
Day Five Comments:	1	2	3	4	5	6	7
Day Six Comments:	1	2	3	4	5	6	7
Day Seven Comments:	1	2	3	4	5	6	7
Day Eight Comments:	1	2	3	4	5	6	7
Day Nine Comments:	1	2	3	4	5	6	7
Day Ten Comments:	1	2	3	4	5	6	7

As performers become more experienced at using relaxation techniques, they can combine PMR with breathing exercises (eg taking slow, rhythmical breaths in time with relaxation and tension) and/or visualisation (eg imagining oneself in a favourite tranquil place while performing PMR). They will also be able to detect any tension in the muscles more easily, and so employ a suitable technique to remove it.[1]

When the tension stems from worrying thoughts or distractions, performers may benefit from mind-to-body relaxation techniques, such as simple meditation, imagery and centering.

Meditation

Meditation allows the performer to relax while simultaneously focusing the mind. It has four main elements:

- A quiet, warm environment (eg changing room, car).
- A comfortable position (eg sitting, lying).
- An object/word on which to focus attention (a mantra).
- A passive attitude, allowing thoughts to pass through the mind, passively returning to the object of focus.

Try the following simple exercise with your performers. This might be done after a training session or the evening before a competition.

---

1 For further help on developing relaxation and emotional control techniques, you are recommended to the **sports coach UK** resource **Handling Pressure**. Available from **Coachwise 1st4sport** (tel: 0113-201 5555 or visit www.1st4sport.com).

ACTIVITY 46

The following instructions represent a simple relaxation script (as is often given in coaching texts). Coaches should be aware that some performers can fall into a deeply relaxed state and in this state may experience unpleasant thoughts or images. If you or performers are concerned about possible reactions, you are recommended to use a professionally prepared audio-tape[1] or, if relaxation is a major concern for your performers, seek the advice of an accredited sports psychologist.

1 Give your performers the following instructions:

- Sit quietly in a comfortable position.
- Close your eyes (you may wish to imagine a non-stimulating object or scene such as a tree, lake or beach).
- Release all the tension from your muscles.
- Concentrating on your breathing, as you breathe out say the word *calm* silently to yourself, breathing naturally (you may wish to use a different word).
- Repeat over a 10–15 minute period.

2 After the session, encourage performers to talk through their feelings and the level of relaxation they were able to gain. Explain that they will become more skilled with practice.

Some performers will find this easier than others. However, with practice, most performers will improve their ability to relax using this technique.

Imagery is another mind-to-body technique which some performers like to use to relax. The aim is to visualise a setting in which the performer feels comfortable and relaxed; typically, sitting in a quiet wood or lying on a deserted beach, listening to the sounds of birds or waves are images which are relaxing. The more senses used by the performer, the more realistic the image and the more relaxed the performer is likely to feel. Calming music can accompany this technique (and be used to associate with a relaxed state).

 Ask your performers to try this relaxation technique the night before competition.

These strategies are useful when performers have time to employ them (eg before or after training or competition, the night before competition). However, performers will often require a *quick fix* technique to increase feelings of relaxation (eg between points, during change overs, during time-outs). **Centering**, a technique which requires the performer to change the centre of consciousness from the head to the centre of gravity (normally a point just below the navel), allows the performer to feel more balanced and stable, and so in control of the situation[1].

---

1   For more details on centering, you are referred to the **sports coach UK** resource **Handling Pressure**. Available from **Coachwise 1st4sport** (tel: 0113-201 5555 or visit www.1st4sport.com).

ACTIVITY 47

1 During your performers' next training session, choose a moment when
   there is a need to relax and refocus. At this moment, ask performers to:

   • imagine their consciousness slipping down from the head, down the neck,
     through the chest and into the stomach, coming to rest just below the navel

   • take a deep breath (using the diaphragm), and as they exhale, focus for a
     moment on this part of the body.

2 Ask each performer to note down how easily they did this:

Performer 1:

Performer 2:

Performer 3:

*Centering allows the performer to relax quickly, and thereby regain control of
situations that are starting to slip away. A deep breath and exhalation, accompanying
a change in the centre of consciousness is often all that is needed to relax and refocus.
It can therefore be used prior to other mental skills practices (eg visualisation prior to
competition). Once again, performers will improve their ability to use this technique
with experience.*

When performers find it easy to centre, they can use this technique in training and
competition whenever they feel it necessary (eg before the start, during half-time,
between routines, when there is a break in the action, at a critical moment in the
score line, after an unfavourable decision, when they have been fouled or injured).

6.4   Anger

Another emotion which is often experienced but sometimes not well controlled is
anger. Channelled, managed aggression can be an asset in some sports but when
control is lost and anger is allowed to boil to the surface, concentration is lost,
mistakes are made, rules are broken and the risk of injury is increased.

Uncontrolled anger.

ACTIVITY 48

Describe occasions when your performers have displayed uncontrolled anger and explain the effect it had on performance:

Occasion: Effect on performance:

•   •

•   •

•   •

Now turn over.

A performer's anger can be provoked by numerous factors. For example:

- *An official's decision*
- *Poor performance by team-mates*
- *Noisy spectators*
- *An opponent who is perceived as aggressive*
- *Poor personal performance*
- *Anxiety*

When performers become angry, this anger often becomes the focus of their attention. It is relatively common to hear of sports performers who allow one bad instance to affect their whole competition. When this happens concentration is lost (because the anger-provoking action becomes the focus), the performer begins to make mistakes and poor decisions (because of this preoccupation), and confidence begins to slip away because of the feeling that things are going wrong.

Look back at Activities 33 (page 91) and 34 (page 93) to check whether you identified anger (or similar emotions) as a distraction.

 Do you ever become angry when coaching or watching an event in which your performers are participating? If so, how do you behave? What effects might this behaviour have on performers?

Cognitive Restructuring

A strategy which can be used to cope with uncontrolled anger is **cognitive restructuring**. This technique is similar to the process of turning negative self-talk into positive self-talk. However, instead of the negative thoughts being directed towards oneself (as in negative self-talk), the anger is aimed at other people or objects. The performer has to learn to accept that problems will occur and the challenge is to overcome them without losing performance.

ACTIVITY 49

1 Putting yourself in the place of the performer, describe how you would deal with each of the following problems:

  • An official's unfavourable decision:

  • Poor performance of a team-mate:

  • Noisy spectators:

  • An opponent perceived as aggressive:

  • Personal poor performance:

2 Add any other situation you (or your performers) find hard to handle in your sport and suggest ways to handle it:

Now turn over.

For each of these, performers need to restructure their thinking so they accept the problem, recognise it could happen to anyone and turn each negative feeling into a challenge.

For the following examples, you might encourage performers to focus on the suggestions given. A word might be used to trigger the restructuring (see trigger words in Activity 36 on page 97).

- *An official's unfavourable decision:*
  Official's decisions average out. Just focus on your own performance.

- *Poor performance by a team-mate:*
  Everyone has an off-day. How can you help and encourage your team-mates?

- *Noisy spectators:*
  All performers have to put up with noisy spectators. See if you can block them out.

- *An opponent who is perceived as aggressive:*
  The opponent is trying to aggravate you. See if you can maintain performance by keeping calm.

- *Personal poor performance:*
  Good performers come back from poor performances to be even better than before. See if you can come back and improve your performance.

6.5 Implications for Your Coaching

It is important to realise that you act as a role model for your performers (especially young performers). If you lose your control and display anxiety or anger, you may provoke similar responses in them (ie anxiety can be contagious).

Even though you may not verbalise this loss of control, non-verbal communication (especially body language) can reveal your emotions. So, whatever the provocation (eg an unfavourable decision by an official), you must learn to control your emotions; you will then be able to help your performers to do the same.

Action Plan

Use the profiling techniques learnt in Chapter Two (page 34) to assess the extent to which your performers experience anxiety and anger (or any other emotions). You may wish to contrast your assessment with that of your performers. For those performers who experience high levels of anxiety or anger, devise an emotional control strategy to help them. Detail the techniques you would use, including a coaching session designed to develop emotional control. Implement this strategy, monitor its progress and evaluate its success.

6.6   Recap and What Next?

All performers experience heightened emotions at some point during their sports participation. This chapter has examined the effects of these emotions on performance. It has focused on two of the most common emotions which can be detrimental to performance and identified techniques which can be used to control them. You have also been given an opportunity to try some of these techniques with your performers.

The following will complement information given in this chapter:

Crisfield, P, Houlston, D and Ledger, P (1996) **Coaching Sessions: A Guide to Planning and Goal-setting.** Leeds, the National Coaching Foundation. ISBN 0 947850 351 X.

The following are suggested for those wishing to develop a greater understanding of topics presented in this chapter:

Harris, D (1986) **Relaxation and energizing techniques for regulation of arousal.** In Williams, JM (ed) Applied sport psychology: personal growth to peak performance. Palo Alto CA, Mayfield. ISBN 076741 747 X.

The following **sports coach UK** workshops may be useful:

Coaching Methods and Communication

Motivation and Mental Toughness

Performance Profiling

For further details contact **sports coach UK** on 0113-274 4802 or visit www.sportscoachuk.org

132

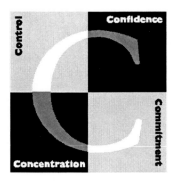

CHAPTER SEVEN

Putting it all Together

Chapter Seven: Putting it all Together

7.0 What's in It For You?

Using the profiling techniques developed in Chapter Two you should now be able to describe the model performer and the levels of each of the mental qualities you would consider necessary for success in your sport. You will also be able to assess each of your performer's current level of these qualities in relation to this model. Where there are significant discrepancies (potential weaknesses), you need to be able to implement an appropriate mental skills strategy to address them. Where performers have the required qualities, a programme which maintains these is necessary.

You should now have a repertoire of techniques on which to draw and have identified a number of ways in which your own behaviour and *management style* can influence your performers' mental approach to sport. Which skills you use and how you use them will depend on the needs of your sport and the mental qualities of your performers. This chapter will help you integrate mental training techniques into your everyday coaching situations and provide advice to performers on how they can use mental skills on competition days. The chapter also provides examples of how top performers have used a variety of mental skills in preparation for and during major competitions.

By the end of this chapter, you should be able to:

- devise a competition-day mental skills routine with one of your performers
- devise an action plan for integrating mental training into your coaching practices
- ensure that your coaching behaviour and the coaching environment support each performer's needs
- identify approximate ages at which each mental skill should be introduced.

7.1 Routines for Competition

The nature of your sport will present performers with specific opportunities to use mental skills before, during and after competition. Certainly, closed skill sports (eg golf, archery) provide breaks in the competitive action which create opportunities to use mental skills. Other sports have elaborate pre-competition routines which only permit the integration of mental skills with careful consideration (eg the time athletes are kept in the holding room prior to a major track and field final).

ACTIVITY 50

Consider a competition day in your sport (the 24 hour period from the night before the competition to the return journey from the venue after the event).

1 List the opportunities to influence the performer's mental qualities over this period (in the left-hand column) and the main mental quality which is required at each of these times (in the right-hand column). You may find it helpful to re-examine your answers to Activities 6 and 7 (on pages 21 and 23).

Time/Opportunity	Mental Quality(s)
eg immediately pre-event	self-confidence

2 In the left-hand column list occasions leading up to and during a competition
   where your behaviour can affect performers' mental preparation (eg increase
   or decrease self-confidence, cause anxiety). In the middle column list the
   mental quality which would be affected (eg emotional control), and in the
   right-hand column suggest ways of changing negative influences into positive
   ones (eg applying relaxation techniques to reduce your own anxiety level).

Occasion	Mental Quality(s)	Action
eg travelling with the performer to the event	self-confidence	using affirmation statements and restating goals for the event

Now turn over.

The physical and psychological training your performers undertake culminates in performance in competition. Performers' mental qualities will be demanded most in the competitive event, with the nature of the sport determining the relative demands placed on each. What follows is an example of the mental qualities which might be needed at different times leading up to, during and after a competitive event:

Time/Opportunity	Mental Quality(s)
Night before	*Ability to relax*
Morning of the event	*Self-confidence, focus*
Warm-up	*Focus/concentration, self-confidence*
Immediately pre-event	*Focus, self-confidence*
During competitive action	*Emotional control, focus*
Breaks in competitive action	*Re-focus, emotional control, self-confidence, concentration*
Post-event	*Self-confidence, emotional control*

Each of these mental qualities contributes to better performance. Therefore, opportunities for developing the appropriate mental skill in training need to be identified. These skills need to be honed so that they can be applied when needed in competition.

Your behaviour can have a major influence on performers' mental preparation and mental state before and during competition. The table below gives some examples.

Occasion	Mental Quality(s)	Action
Travelling with the performer to the event	Self-confidence	Using affirmation statements and restating goals for the event.
On arrival at the venue	Emotional control	Taking care of performer's needs (eg checking competition details) to reduce anxiety, maintain own emotional control, be positive.
During warm-up	Concentration	Avoid providing irrelevant or too much information, keep comments simple.
At half-time	Self-confidence and concentration	Make comments constructive, focus on key goals for second half. Encourage.
During action (if able to communicate verbally or non-verbally)	Emotional control and concentration	Maintain own emotional control. Keep communications simple.

Stephen Ward, British Weightlifting Champion

When about to lift, it is essential that Ward concentrates solely on what he is doing and avoids distractions. Ward uses visualisation to improve his concentration. His coach and sports psychologist encourage him to picture and feel his best lifts, using appropriate music to associate with these pictures and feelings. This music can then be played in training and during warm-up to help concentrate on the lift ahead.

The Contenders, BBC Video

Visualisation can improve concentration.

Work through the next activity to identify which skills are most needed at each point during competition.

ACTIVITY 51

Consider the constraints placed on performers at each of the times identified in Activity 50 on page 136 (eg during the 15 minutes immediately prior to competition, performers might be kept together in a waiting area). Considering the mental skills developed in this pack, list in the right-hand column the most appropriate skill(s) to use at each of these times (for as many mental qualities as you feel appropriate).

Time/Opportunity	Mental Quality(ies)	Mental Skill(s)
Night before	Ability to relax	
Morning of the event	Self-confidence Focus	
Warm-up	Focus/concentration Self-confidence	
Immediately pre-event	Focus Self-confidence	
During competitive action	Emotional control Focus	
Breaks in competitive action	Re-focus Emotional control Self-confidence Concentration	
Post-event	Self-confidence Emotional control	

Now turn over.

What follows is an example of how some mental skills can be used before, during and after competition:

Time/Opportunity	Mental Quality(ies)	Mental Skill(s)
Night before	Ability to relax	PMR
Morning of the event	Self-confidence	Positive affirmation (self-talk) Cognitive restructuring Imagery (mental rehearsal)
	Focus	Goal re-statement Routines Crib cards
Warm-up	Focus/Concentration Self-confidence	Centering Positive self-talk Mental rehearsal
Immediately pre-event	Focus	Mental rehearsal Trigger words Positive self-talk
	Self-confidence	Positive self-talk Mental rehearsal
During competitive action	Emotional control Focus	Cognitive restructuring Trigger words
Breaks in competitive action	Re-focus	Centering + trigger words
	Emotional control Self-confidence Concentration	Cognitive restructuring Mental rehearsal Mental rehearsal + trigger words + positive self-talk
Post-event	Self-confidence	Goal appraisal/ goal setting Visualisation (mental review)
	Emotional control	Cognitive re-structuring

If you are unsure of how to use any of these mental skills, go back to the relevant section in this pack and work through it again.

Angela Chalmers, Bronze Medallist, 1992 Olympic Games, Womens 3000m.

The day before the 3000m heats, Wynn (coach) and I pulled out the race prep notebook (prepared prior to the Games). We looked at the women in my heat and planned the race accordingly. I was very relaxed and confident when I lined up for my race. In the final minutes before the gun went off I repeated a few of the key words I wanted to use in the race...

(During the race) I regained my composure by repeating my key words and reminding myself that I was tough, strong and relaxed.

Chalmers, 1994[1]

7.2 Implications for Your Coaching

You need to be aware of all the opportunities for helping performers mentally prepare for competition and applying mental skills on competition day. You also need to be aware of your potential for negative influence.

 Consider each of the following in relation to your sport:

- What do you see as your role on competition day?

- What sorts of things do you discuss with performers immediately prior to an event?

- How do you react when something goes wrong at an event (eg the performer loses piece of equipment needed for the event)?

- How do you relax before and during a competition?

- On what do you focus at half-time or during breaks in the action (if this is applicable to your sport)?

- How soon after the event do you discuss the outcome with performers?

- How do you deal with a performer's loss of self-confidence on the day of a competition?

- What message does your body language give at a competition?

Questions like these should help you analyse your own coaching behaviour. This is the first step to ensuring you maintain a positive influence on your performers.

---

1 In Access to Active Living (pp424–429), Proceedings of the 10th Commonwealth and International Scientific Congress, 10–14 August 1994, University of Victoria, Canada.

7.3   Integrating Mental Skills into Your Coaching

You should now have identified the potential for influencing performers' mental qualities. This section will help you translate the opportunities identified in the previous activities into coaching practice.

ACTIVITY 52

Look back at Activity 11 (on page 28, which identifies the mental qualities needed by your performers). You should now be able to list below the mental skills necessary to develop these qualities:

Mental Qualities (from Activity 11)	Mental Skills

Once you have prioritised which mental skills are key for a particular performer, you will need to devise ways of developing them in training.

Scottish Women's Bowls Team, World Team Champions

For the women's bowls team, feeling in control of the competitive situation and remaining confident are essential for success. The sports psychologist and team manager helped the bowlers adopt a more positive attitude to team competitions by encouraging supporting players to display dominant body language (eg standing over the jack with hands on hips). This supported the bowler and gave the impression to opponents of team confidence. This supportive behaviour was developed in training.

The Contenders, BBC Video

The following panel provides some practical examples of mental skills sessions which can be integrated into a coaching programme. They are given to help you identify the potential for developing these skills (and are not meant to suggest a priority for your coaching practices).

Integrated mental skills training sessions

The following exercises are given as examples of mental skills training. In completing the subsequent activities, you will need to adapt these exercises to meet the needs of your performers.

Exercise 1

To help performers relax in situations where they are prone to become tense
(eg when about to serve, when waiting to bowl in cricket, before taking a penalty).

The development of this mental skill is in two stages:

- Developing the skill in training.

- Integrating the skill within a competition-specific performance routine.

1 The following instructions are given to performers to use each day for one month (usually last thing at night or during a quiet time during the day):

  - Begin by centering.

  - Visualise yourself in a competitive situation just before you usually become tense (eg a tennis serve).

  - While experiencing the scene, become aware of the relaxed feelings you experienced when centering (as you do so, repeat a word which evokes these feelings of relaxation – examples of this trigger word might be *relax* or *calm*).

  - If you feel tension increasing, end your visualisation and center again.

  - When relaxation has been regained, visualise the scene again, using your trigger word to help stay relaxed.

  - Once you feel relaxed, see and feel yourself take a deep breath, say your relaxation trigger word, and perform the activity successfully.

  - Repeat this exercise until you no longer sense any tension.

2 After about a month (or when performers feel they can relax when visualising), ask them to use centering and their trigger word before competition-specific elements in training. Once performers have integrated this skill into training, it can be used at key competitive moments.

ACTIVITY 53

Based on Exercise 1

Look back at your performers' priorities for developing mental skills (based on the information in Activity 11, on page 28). If relaxation is one mental quality in need of improvement, this activity may be particularly relevant. During the early part of the season, ask one of your performers to spend 10–15 minutes each day running through the previously described relaxation script (Exercise 1 in panel) and use the trigger word in competition. Repeat this over a four or five week period. Ask the performer to rate the effectiveness of this mental training in reducing tension at important moments in competition and training, using the scale below.

Effectiveness of this mental skill:

Not effective   Very effective

| 1 | 2 | 3 | 4 | 5 |

Use of this rating scale should be repeated throughout the season to monitor progress.

Initially, some performers may not feel that mental skills work for them. If you or your performers feel this technique to be ineffective, encourage performers to try another trigger word or identify a visual cue which can evoke a relaxed state. Use the principles in the example to find the most effective way for this performer to relax.

Integrated mental skills training sessions

Exercise 2

To develop the skill of changing from a narrow external to a broad external focus of attention (the example given is in soccer, where a player may need to switch focus from the ball to team-mates and opponents)[1].

This practice will require four players and a soccer ball, and is conducted in the following formation:

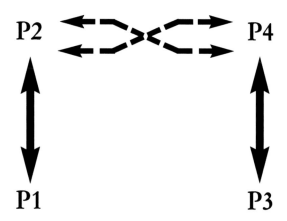

P1 passes the ball to P2, who returns the pass. Simultaneously, P3 does the same with P4. P2 and P4 then switch attention to each other, switch positions, avoiding contact as they do so. They then receive and give passes from the new partner (ie P1 passes to P4, who passes back; P3 passes to P2, who passes back). This continues with players switching attention from ball, to moving player, to ball.

---

1   This practice was first published in Mace, R (1995) **With netball in mind**. It is reproduced with permission of the author. More examples of attentional focus training are given in this text.

ACTIVITY 54

Based on Exercise 2

Using Exercise 2 as a template, go back to Activity 32 on page 89 and examine the attentional demands of your sport. Design a training session or practice which helps performers develop an appropriate attentional focus to meet the demands of a typically stressful or decision-making situation in your sport:

Your session should reflect the attentional demands of your sport and provide the performer(s) with opportunities to perform sport-specific activities which create and concentrate on these demands. If your sport utilises a variety of attentional states, these should be re-created in the session (preferably in a manner similar to competitive situations).

Integrated mental skills training sessions

Exercise 3

To maintain self-confidence during the pre-competition period leading to the start of the event.

Each performer develops a competition-day routine which includes time for:

- goal re-statements to remind the performer of, and reaffirm the key objectives for, the competition (eg performers spend time after breakfast reminding themselves of their competition goals; these may be written down for competition evaluation after the event)

- mental rehearsal of successful performances in a range of situations which the performer may face in the competition (eg on the team bus, performers visualise a range of successful performances)

- positive affirmation statements (eg during the warm-up period, performers make positive self-statements such as *use my power*) which focus on the qualities most needed for the event.

ACTIVITY 55

Based on Exercise 3

Identify a performer you coach who suffers from losses of self-confidence immediately prior to competition (it may help to re-examine Activity 21 on page 60). With this performer, develop a routine for the next competition which includes goal re-statements, mental rehearsal and positive affirmation statements. Encourage this performer to use the routine and assess its worth after the competition. You may wish to ask the performer the following questions and use the marking scale 1 (not at all) to 5 (very easily/much):

- To what extent was it easy to find the time to work through this routine on the day of the competition?

  1   2   3   4   5

- To what extent did re-stating your goals help clarify (and achieve) your targets for the competition?

  1   2   3   4   5

- To what extent did mental rehearsal give you confidence to cope with any competition occurrences?

  1   2   3   4   5

- To what extent did making positive affirmation statements boost your confidence?

  1   2   3   4   5

The responses to these questions will vary between performers. If performers find any of these techniques ineffective, you may need to work through the process again to check the techniques are being effectively used. If necessary, work through the section on self-confidence again, in order to adapt the routine to meet this performer's needs. For example, you may wish to develop further this performer's visualisation skills in training.

This pack will have helped you to identify the mental skills needed by performers to plan and implement mental skills training in ways which they can directly apply to competitive situations. Your success will hinge on assessing individual needs.

You will probably have identified ways in which you can integrate simple mental skills into everyday coaching practice (eg concentration drills, routines prior to specific situations). This type of training can be used with all performers irrespective of age. However, there are guidelines for developing more specialist mental skills with adolescents and children. If you coach performers of varying ages and maturity, the table below provides a basic guideline to help identify at which ages specialist mental skills can be introduced.

Area	Programme	Suggested Starting Age (Years)
Mental conditioning	Muscular and mental relaxation	9
Mental technique training	Imagery training	9
Mental strength training	Mental skills acquisition: Concentration	12
	Motivation training: Goal-setting	15
	Attitude training: Cognitive structuring (positive thinking)	9
	Self-confidence training	12
	Cognitive restructuring	15

Suggested ages for the introduction of mental skills
Adapted from Gordin, Unesthal, Henschen and Sands, 1987

If you or your performers wish to develop further some of the skills introduced in this pack, the **sports coach UK** programme of mental skills resources (see page 154) and the workshops **Performance Profiling** and **Imagery Training** may help you do this.

By now you have probably decided what action you are going take to adjust your coaching behaviour and help develop performers' mental skills. With the principles of effective goal-setting in mind, use the remaining two activities to set a realistic goal for making positive changes to your coaching and developing the mental skills of one of your performers.

ACTIVITY 56

Choose one aspect of your coaching behaviour which you feel might (on occasions) negatively influence the performance of one of your performers. Explain why you think it occurs and when it is most likely to happen. Describe a goal for improving this behaviour and the action (eg use of mental skills) you will take to achieve it. Explain how you will monitor improvements in your behaviour.

Aspect:

•

When:

•

Outcome:

•

Goal (S M A R T):

•

Time frame:

•

Monitor:

•

ACTIVITY 57

For one of your performers, set a goal (or goals) to develop appropriate mental skills (if you have profiled this performer earlier in the pack, refer back to this profile before completing the activity). Detail which skills you will develop, how and when you will develop them, how you will monitor the effectiveness of the programme, and the intended effects on competition performance:

Performance:

•

Skill:

•

How:

•

When:

•

Monitor:

•

Effects on competitive performance:

•

You should use these activities as the starting point for implementing a personal development plan and improving your performer's mental skills. If at any point you have difficulty with this programme, refer back to the relevant section in the pack or consult some of the further reading material. More detailed advice may be sought from an accredited sports psychologist[1].

7.4   What Next?

If you would like further information, the following courses and books may be useful:

Butler, R (1991) **Amateur boxing and sports science II: psychology.** *Coaching Focus*, No 18 Winter, pp14–15. Leeds, the National Coaching Foundation. ISSN 0267–4416.

---

1   Details of the services provided by accredited sports psychologists are included in Appendix B (page 159).

Cox, R (2000) **Sports psychology: concepts and applications** (4th edition).*
New York, McGraw-Hill. ISBN 0 07250 525 7.

Gallwey, T (1997) **Inner game of tennis. (Revised ed.)** New York, Random House.
ISBN 0 67977 831 4.

Morris, T and Bull S J (1991) **Mental training in sport: an overview.** (BASES
Monograph No 3).

National Coaching Foundation (1996) **Coaching Sessions: A Guide to Planning and
Goal-setting.** Leeds, National Coaching Foundation. ISBN 0 947850 35 X.

National Coaching Foundation (1997) **Building Self Confidence**
Leeds, National Coaching Foundation. ISBN 0 947850 11 2.

National Coaching Foundation (1998) **Imagery Training**
Leeds, National Coaching Foundation. ISBN 0 902523 10 5.

National Coaching Foundation (1998) **Improving Concentration**
Leeds, National Coaching Foundation. ISBN 0 902523 01 6.

National Coaching Foundation (1998) **Handling Pressure**
Leeds, National Coaching Foundation. ISBN 0 902523 09 1

National Coaching Foundation (1999) **Motivation and Mental Toughness**
Leeds, National Coaching Foundation. ISBN 0 902523 24 5.

Orlick, T (1990) **In pursuit of excellence: how to win in sport and life through
mental training (3rd Edition).** Champaign, IL, Human Kinetics. ISBN 0 73603 186 3.

Butler, R (1996) **Performance profiling.** (Tape and booklet.) Leeds, the National
Coaching Foundation

The following **sports coach UK** workshops may be useful:

Coaching Methods and Communication

Goal-Setting and Planning

Motivation and Mental Toughness

Performance Profiling

For further details contact **sports coach UK** on 0113-274 4802 or visit
www.sportscoachuk.org

* Available from **Coachwise 1st4sport,** (tel: 0113-201 5555 or visit www.1st4sport.com).

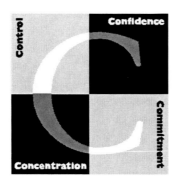

APPENDIX A

Glossary of Terms

Appendix A: Glossary of Terms

Affirmation statements:	words you say to yourself that reflect and reinforce positive attitudes or thoughts
Anger:	an emotion sometimes expressed as uncontrolled aggression
Anxiety:	a subjective feeling of apprehension
Arousal:	a general physiological state which can range from extreme calm to extreme excitement
Attentional focus:	those internal and external cues to which the performer is paying attention
Attentional style:	the tendency to adopt a particular attentional focus
Centering:	a technique for regaining focus and relaxation by changing the centre of consciousness from the head to the centre of gravity (a point just below the navel)
Cognitive anxiety:	negative thoughts about performance
Cognitive restructuring:	a means of changing negative thoughts into positive ones, to enhance self-confidence and reduce anxiety
Commitment:	the ability to continue striving for agreed goals in training and competition despite distractions
Concentration:	the ability to maintain attentional focus
Control (emotional):	the ability to maintain an appropriate emotional state regardless of internal and external influences
Crib cards:	written reminders to aid performance
Distraction training:	training designed to help the performer overcome the distractions present in the sport
Goal-setting:	the process by which the coach and performer agree short-, medium- and long-term targets
Imagery:	using the senses to recreate an image of a desired action or state
Meditation:	a technique for enhancing relaxation which involves focusing on a word, phrase or image in order to alter the mind from an active to a passive state
Mental quality:	a state of mind which enhances performance

Mental skill:	the application of appropriate psychological techniques to enhance performance
Performance profiling:	a technique for identifying and contrasting strengths and weaknesses
Positive self-talk:	using positive statements to develop self-confidence
Process goal:	a target which indicates what the performer has to do in order to be successful
Product goal:	a target which indicates an end result, either in terms of a comparison with other performers (outcome goal) or with an absolute standard (performance goal)
Progressive Muscular Relaxation:	the body to mind method of systematic tensing and relaxing groups of muscles
Routines:	a customary sequence of predetermined behaviours
Segmenting:	the process of dividing into identifiable sub-components
Self-confidence:	a general belief in one's ability
Somatic anxiety:	a negative interpretation of a physiological state
Stress:	the non-specific response of the mind and body to any demand made upon it; can be either positive or negative
Trigger word:	a word which stimulates a specific response

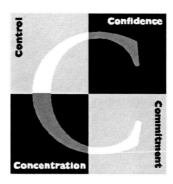

APPENDIX B

Advice to Clients of Sport and Exercise Psychology Services

Appendix B: Advice to Clients of Sport and Exercise Psychology Services

For Distribution to Clients

Working practice in sport and exercise psychology support

This document briefly outlines the standards of service that you, the client, may expect from an accredited sport and exercise psychologist or someone who is undergoing supervised experience to become accredited. It includes the general expectations and methods of working which have been approved by the Psychology Section of the British Association of Sport and Exercise Sciences (BASES). There is also a brief description of the complaints procedure which is open to you if you are not satisfied with the quality of service you receive.

Also attached is a Support Service pro forma. Section 1 should be completed by your potential sport and exercise psychologist to provide you with some information about his/her previous experience. This pro forma will form the basis of the contractual agreement between yourself and the sport and exercise psychologist if you decide that he/she can help you.

Standards of Service
The sport and exercise psychologist will indicate to you on the pro forma whether or not he/she is accredited or in the process of supervised experience. Note that accredited individuals are limited to work within their scope of expertise; in addition, accreditation can be for research or for support work. Therefore, the psychologist will indicate his or her areas of expertise to you before agreeing to a programme of work.

An accredited sport and exercise psychologist has been through a quality assurance process which requires him/her to meet a number of required criteria, go through a peer review of theoretical expertise and a period of supervised experience of up to three years. An accredited sport and exercise psychologist has developed areas of competence within which he/she is expected to remain. A Code of Conduct governs the good practice of all sport and exercise psychologists and failure to observe such good and established practice results in the individual being answerable to the Executive Committee of BASES.

A sport and exercise psychologist who is in the process of supervised experience will be working under the direct supervision of a support accredited sport and exercise psychologist.

A support accredited sport and exercise psychologist can offer you a number of different services. These include education, which involves the delivery of educational material in a number of different forms, and support for effective exercise environments or performance enhancement, which may include any of a number of intervention strategies employed to facilitate improvements in a variety of mental and physical factors.

General expectations and complaints procedure
You, the client, should be made aware at the outset that the sport and exercise psychologist must preserve confidentiality and have your informed consent before undertaking any work. You may expect the sport and exercise psychologist to negotiate the boundaries of confidentiality at an early stage to confirm who is involved, and to what degree, in your support network (eg coach, selector, physiotherapist, manager). In other words, the psychologist must clarify with you, the client, who can know what and abide by this agreement unless you give direct permission to the contrary.

There should be a definite logic and rationale for each part of any proposed work, which should be communicated to those involved. As re-evaluation and updating of strategies or methods occurs, the logic and rational should be stated. The provision of such information should enable you to evaluate the suitability of the stated objectives and the strategies or methods employed. Thus you should have an informed choice throughout, and play a full part in decisions on the focus of the intervention work. This should also enable you to monitor your own progress with reference to the objectives. This process should ensure that interventions are personalised and specific to your needs.

The sports psychologist should be working to a situation where he/she makes him/herself redundant, such that you have been educated in the principles of the strategies and methods employed and the relative success of the interventions should be conducted. Of course, at that time you may decide to continue with or extend the scope of the work. Not withstanding this however, the psychologist is duty bound to promote your skills to a level where you can perform without his or her direct help.

If at any point during the process of working with a sport and exercise psychologist you have reason to complain, or think that the BASES Code of Conduct is being breached, please do not hesitate to contact the General Secretary, British Association of Sport and Exercise Sciences, Chelsea Close, Off Amberley Road, Armley, Leeds, LS12 4HP. Tel: 0113-289 1020. By doing this when a member has failed to perform to the high standards required by BASES helps us to maintain quality and protects you and your fellow performers against inept or under-committed service.

Methods of Working

The sport and exercise psychologist should provide you (the client) with the partially completed pro forma which indicates his/her accreditation status, previous experience, and areas of expertise. Assuming you are happy with the information provided, the sport and exercise psychologist would then normally either observe you in a training/competitive environment or have a face-to-face meeting. Following this there should be an evaluation of needs which should include:

- negotiation of the aims and objectives of the service offered
- a discussion of the proposed methods to be employed
- agreement on the proposed scope of these methods, the form of the intervention, the expected outcomes, the time frame, and the costs.

When these details have been agreed, the pro forma may be completed and copies made for all those concerned (eg sport and exercise psychologist, performer, coach, management team). It should be noted that the distribution of the completed pro forma must preserve the agreed confidentiality. Completion of this form is your decision – if completed it does serve as a record of the contractual agreement between you and your psychologist.

The aims, objectives and methods employed should be continually re-evaluated during the support period and, if necessary, updated. The methods should include an outline of the proposed number of contact sessions required for appropriate provision of the service and the costs of such a schedule.

By permission of BASES (Psychology Section)

Sport and Exercise Psychology Support Service Pro forma

1 To be completed by the sport and exercise psychologist.

Name ....

Address..

....

....

Telephone .... BASES Memb No..............................

Accreditation status: Accredited Research   Yes ☐   No ☐

Accredited Support   Yes ☐   No ☐

Supervised Experience   Yr1 ☐   Yr2 ☐   Yr3 ☐

Brief Résumé of Previous Experience

Sports Worked With: Standard of Performer (eg junior, club):

....

....

....

Areas of Expertise:

....

....

....

2 To be completed by client and sport and exercise psychologist.

Name of Client..

Address..

....

.... Telephone ....

Others involved in sport: Role: Telephone:

i)   ....

ii) ....

iii) ....

iv) ....

Agreed Programme of Support ....

Aims and Objectives of service:

....

....

....

Methods to be employed (provide dates to coincide with specific reasons):

....

....

....

Methods of evaluation (provide dates where appropriate):

....

....

....

Proposed number of contact sessions ....

Costs...

Travel and accommodation ....

Consultancy fee...

The proposed programme indicated above is agreed to by the undersigned.

Client   Date

....

Sport and exercise psychologist   Date

....

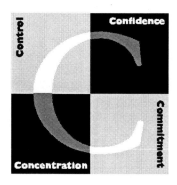

APPENDIX C

Performance Profiles

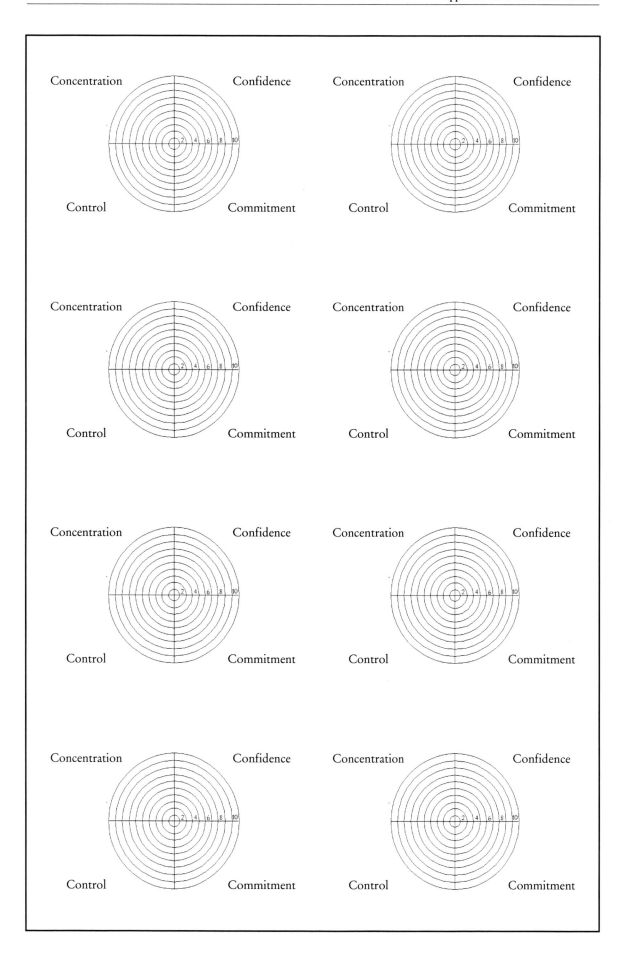

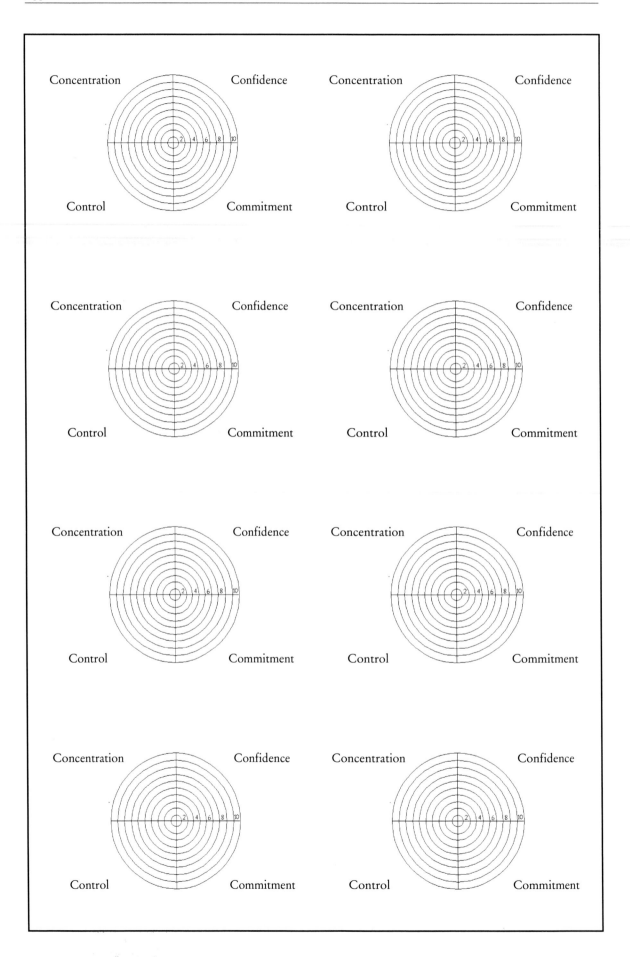

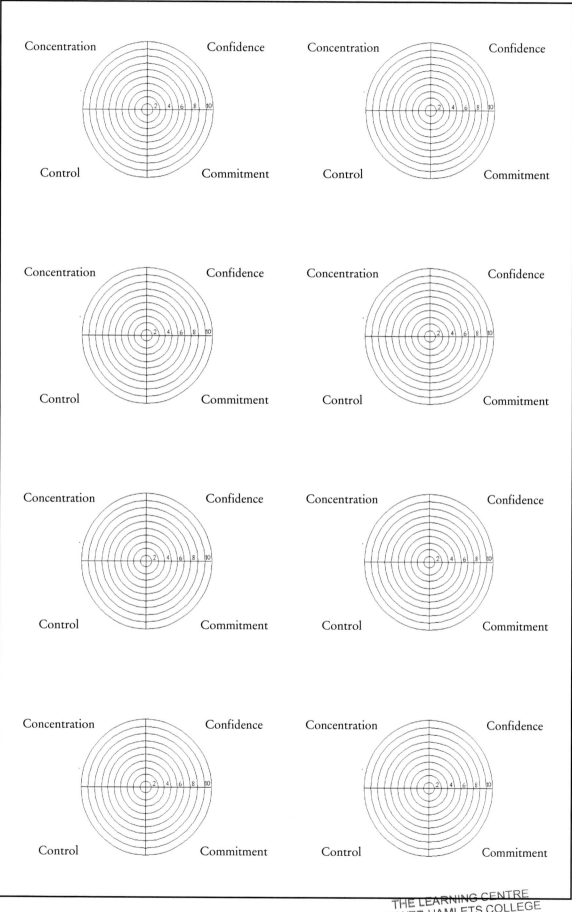

THE LEARNING CENTRE
TOWER HAMLETS COLLEGE
POPLAR CENTRE
POPLAR HIGH STREET
LONDON E14 0AF

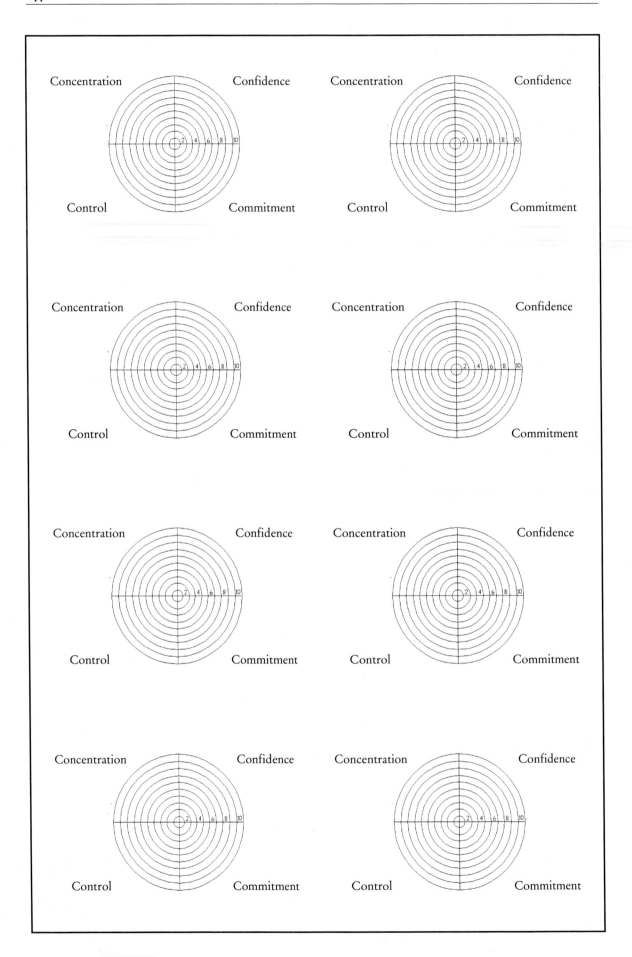